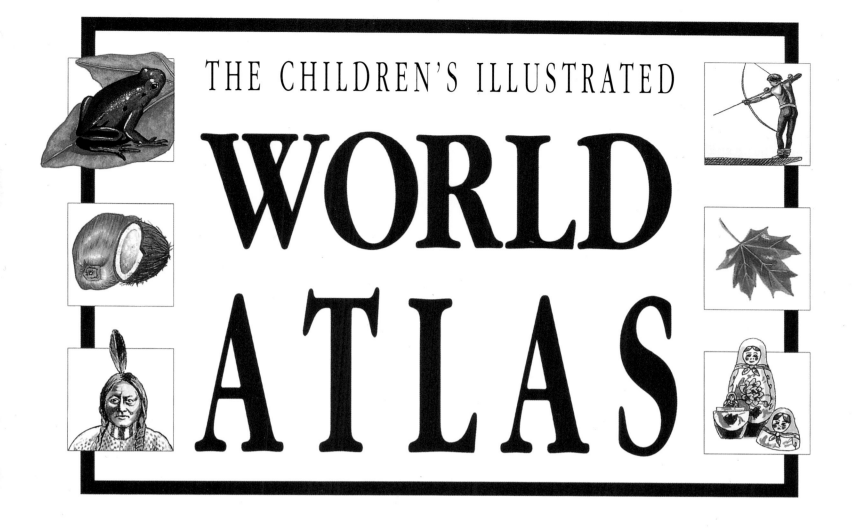

THE CHILDREN'S ILLUSTRATED
WORLD ATLAS

**Molly Perham
and
Philip Steele**

COURAGE
BOOKS
An Imprint of
Running Press
Philadelphia, Pennsylvania

CONTENTS

A Templar Book

Copyright © 1992, 1993 by The Templar Company plc
Devised and produced by The Templar Company plc
Pippbrook Mill, London Road, Dorking, Surrey RH4 1JE, Great Britain.

This edition published in the United States by Courage Books,
an imprint of Running Press Book Publishers.

9 8 7 6 5 4 3 2
Digit on the right indicates the number of this printing.

Library of Congress Cataloging-in-publication Number 93–70591

ISBN 1–56138–331–7

Editor: Wendy Madgwick
Designer: Janie Louise Hunt
Artists: Ann Savage and David Ashby, Alan Baker, Rod Ferring, James Field, Chris Forsey, John Green, Adam Hook, Lorna Hussey, Wendy and Clifford Meadway, David Moore, Sallie Reason, Stella Stilwell, Joyce Tuhill, Avril Turner, Helen Ward

Color separations by Positive Colour Ltd., Maldon, Essex, Great Britain.
Printed in Hong Kong
Cartography and text and illustrations on page 3 by Lovell Johns Ltd., Witney, Oxon, Great Britain.
All photographs supplied by Frank Lane Picture Agency, in conjunction with Silvestris and Colorific!, Pages Green House, Wetheringsett, Stowmarket, Suffolk IP14 5QA, Great Britain.

Published by Courage Books, an imprint of
Running Press Book Publishers
125 South Twenty-Second Street
Philadelphia, Pennsylvania 19103

SCALES and SYMBOLS

Scales

To be of any use, maps have to reduce or scale-down what they represent. Scale is the ratio between the distance on the map and the distance on the ground. A map the same size as the object being drawn is known as a one to one, that is it is drawn at a 1:1 scale. This scale is only useful for really detailed engineering drawings of small objects.

If the scale is 1:1,000,000 then one inch of map represents 1,000,000 inches (15.8 miles) on the ground. If the scale is 1:30,000,000 one inch now represents 30,000,000 inches (473.5 miles). The scale becomes smaller as the number of inches gets bigger.

Maps and Scales

For the purposes of mapping our surroundings, the largest scale normally used would be 1:1,000 (one to one thousand). At this scale the streets around your house, the sidewalk and even the shed in the backyard could be shown accurately. These large-scale maps are usually produced by the official mapping organization of a country. From these maps, others are drawn at smaller scales.

Smaller scale maps can show a larger area of a country on the same size of paper. At a scale of 1:1,000 the area shown on a map may only be about 55,562 square yards (.017 sq. miles); at a scale of 1:20,000 the area covered would be 22,152,300 square yards (7.1 sq. miles). If the scale is reduced still further to 1:100,000, then 55,440,650 square yards (178.7 sq. miles) can be shown.

Whenever you use a map, the scale is one of the first things to look for. It is usually printed somewhere at the edge of the map. Most of the maps in this atlas have scales between 1:5,000,000 and 1:40,000,000. At these scales whole countries can be shown on a page.

A scale bar, a horizontal line divided into sections, is another way of showing the scale of a map. If you take a ruler and measure a distance on the map you can then work out the exact distance in real life using the scale bar.

Using different scales

The maps on the right show the same city, Bombay, but at different scales. Map 1 is the largest scale and Map 3 the smallest.
In Map 1, the roads in Bombay can be shown. You can measure these roads by using the scale bar.
In Map 2, Bombay is shown by a spot. You can measure how far Bombay is from nearby towns by using the scale bar.
In Map 3, the position of Bombay within India can be seen. You can measure how far Bombay is from the other side of India by using the scale bar.

Map 1
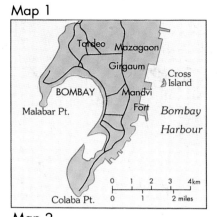

Map 2

Map 3

Symbols

Symbols are used on maps to represent features on the ground. They are not usually drawn to scale and may often be exaggerated in size in order to show something that is important. Three main types of symbols are used on maps. Point symbols show such features as mountain peaks, towns, airports, and waterfalls. Line symbols show such features as international boundaries, roads, rivers, and railways. Area symbols show such features as natural vegetation and land use.

The symbols used in this atlas are shown on pages 12-13. The various symbols shown below are examples of symbols used in other atlases, maps, and tourist guides.

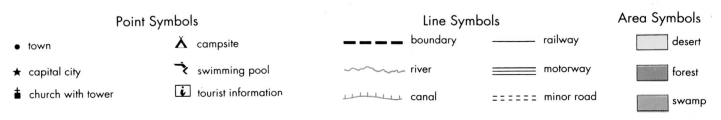

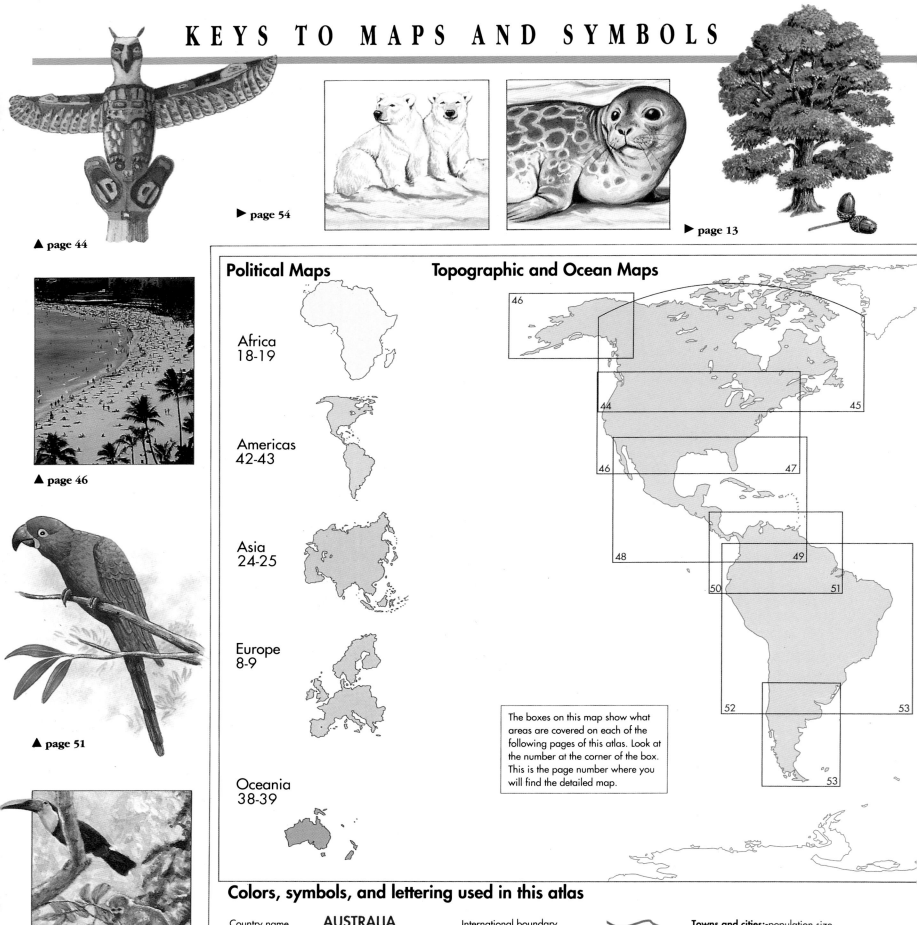

▲ page 44

▶ page 54

▶ page 13

▲ page 46

▲ page 51

▲ page 53

Political Maps

Africa
18-19

Americas
42-43

Asia
24-25

Europe
8-9

Oceania
38-39

Topographic and Ocean Maps

46

44

45

46

47

48

49

50

51

52

53

53

The boxes on this map show what areas are covered on each of the following pages of this atlas. Look at the number at the corner of the box. This is the page number where you will find the detailed map.

Colors, symbols, and lettering used in this atlas

Country name	**AUSTRALIA**	International boundary	
Dependency	**French Guiana**	International boundary, undefined or disputed	
Possession	(Ecuador)	International boundary, at sea	
State or province	QUEENSLAND	Between 100,000 and 500,000 people	
Capital city	WELLINGTON	State or province boundary	
Other city or town	Auckland	State or province boundary, at sea	
Land feature	Nubian Desert C. Agulhas	Equator	
Water feature	L. Taupo Volga	Tropic or polar circle	

Towns and cities:-population size

More than 1,000,000 people ●

Between 500,000 and 1,000,000 people ◉

Between 100,000 and 500,000 people •

Less than 100,000 people ○

Physical features:-

Mountain peak ▲ Mt. Everest 8,848 m

Depression on land ▼ Qattara Depression - 133 m

Depth at sea • Challenger Deep - 10,915 m

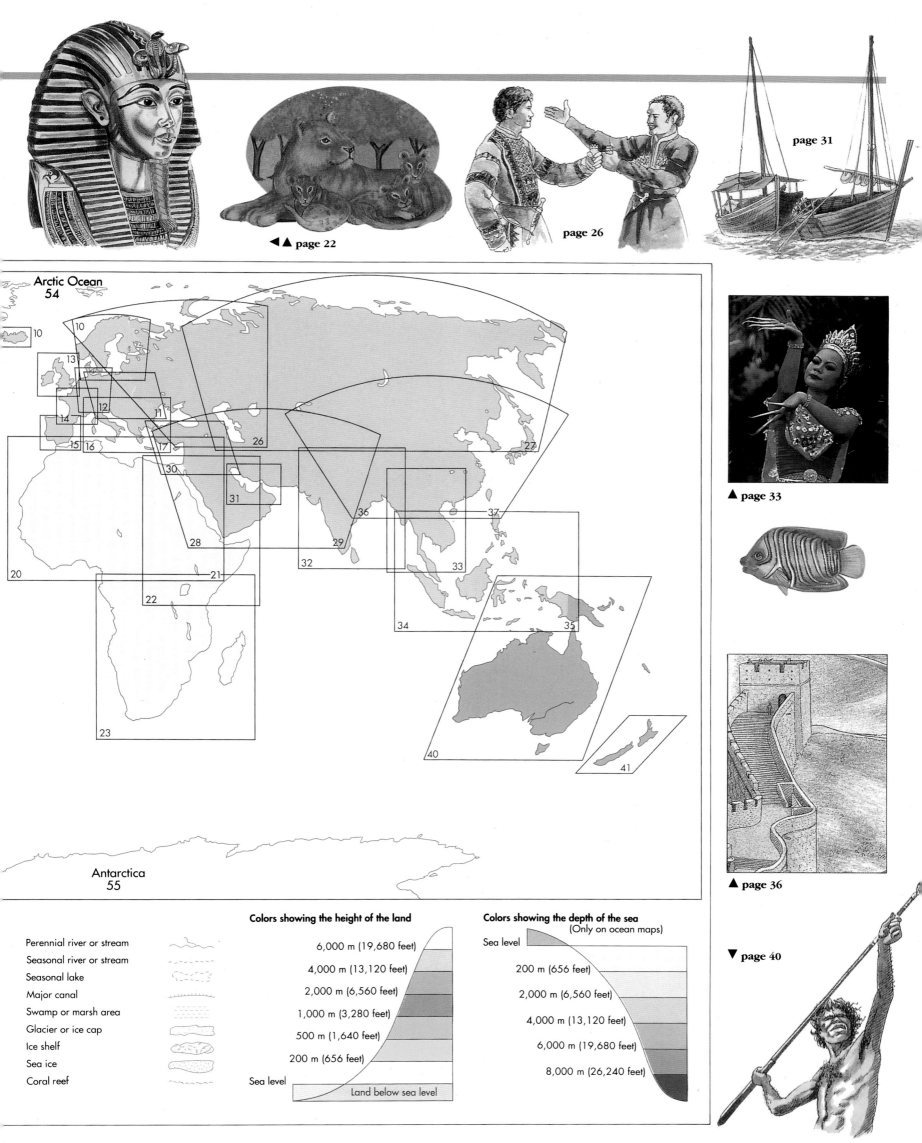

page 31

▼▲ page 22

page 26

▲ page 33

▲ page 36

▼ page 40

Arctic Ocean
54

10
10
13
14
12
11
15
16
17
30
31
28
26
20
21
22
29
32
33
36
37
27
34
35
23
40
41

Antarctica
55

Perennial river or stream
Seasonal river or stream
Seasonal lake
Major canal
Swamp or marsh area
Glacier or ice cap
Ice shelf
Sea ice
Coral reef

Colors showing the height of the land

6,000 m (19,680 feet)
4,000 m (13,120 feet)
2,000 m (6,560 feet)
1,000 m (3,280 feet)
500 m (1,640 feet)
200 m (656 feet)
Sea level

Land below sea level

Colors showing the depth of the sea
(Only on ocean maps)

Sea level
200 m (656 feet)
2,000 m (6,560 feet)
4,000 m (13,120 feet)
6,000 m (19,680 feet)
8,000 m (26,240 feet)

Different types of climate and vegetation divide the world into distinct natural regions. The polar regions are always cold and mainly dry, so that few plants can survive. Temperate climates range from the hot, dry summers and mild winters of the Mediterranean to the cooler, wetter climates of Northern Europe. Plants and animals have adapted to the seasonal changes. Tropical zones are wet and warm with abundant vegetation.

Polar Tundra
In the polar tundra of Alaska, northern Canada, and Siberia, the ground is frozen for much of the year. Only lichens, mosses, and small plants can survive. These flower in the short summer (see right).

Woodland and Meadows
Deciduous forests once covered most of the cool, temperate regions. The trees were felled to provide farming and building land. In parts only woodland and meadows remain (see above).

Tropical Savanna
Between the tropical rain forest and desert regions lie large stretches of grassland called savanna. There is a wet, rainy season, followed by periods of drought.

Deserts
Deserts cover over a quarter of the land surface. Some are hot and sandy; others are cold and rocky. All have very little rain and few plants grow.

Rain Forests
Countries close to the Equator have a hot climate and heavy rainfall all year. Trees and plants grow quickly and provide habitats for a rich variety of animal life.

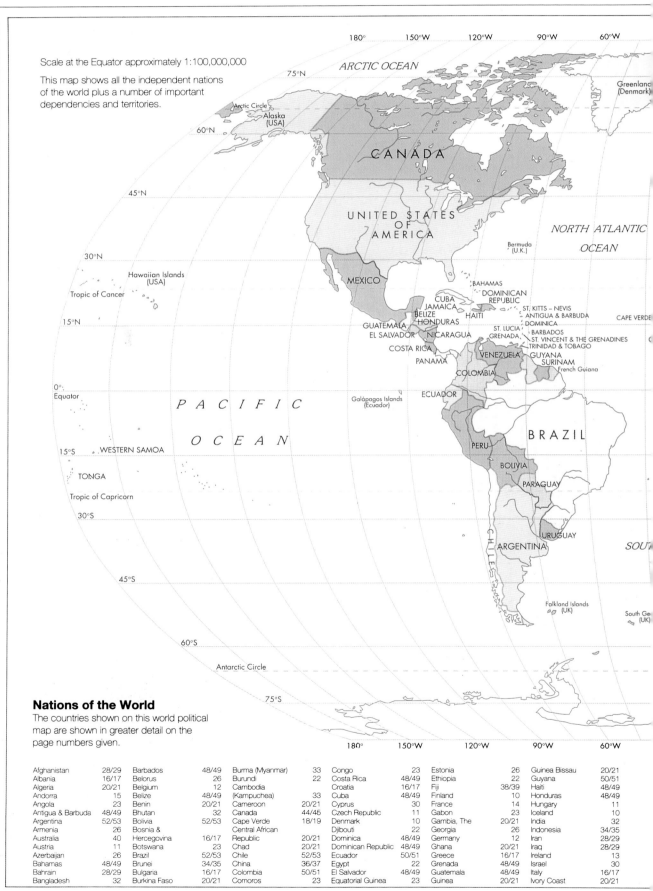

Scale at the Equator approximately 1:100,000,000

This map shows all the independent nations of the world plus a number of important dependencies and territories.

Nations of the World
The countries shown on this world political map are shown in greater detail on the page numbers given.

Map labels: ARCTIC OCEAN, 75°N, 60°N, 45°N, 30°N, 15°N, 0° Equator, 15°S, 30°S, 45°S, 60°S, 75°S, Tropic of Cancer, Tropic of Capricorn, Arctic Circle, Antarctic Circle, 180°, 150°W, 120°W, 90°W, 60°W

CANADA, UNITED STATES OF AMERICA, Alaska (USA), Greenland (Denmark), NORTH ATLANTIC OCEAN, Bermuda (U.K.), Hawaiian Islands (USA), MEXICO, BAHAMAS, CUBA, JAMAICA, HAITI, DOMINICAN REPUBLIC, ST. KITTS – NEVIS, ANTIGUA & BARBUDA, DOMINICA, ST. LUCIA, BARBADOS, ST. VINCENT & THE GRENADINES, GRENADA, TRINIDAD & TOBAGO, CAPE VERDE, BELIZE, GUATEMALA, HONDURAS, EL SALVADOR, NICARAGUA, COSTA RICA, PANAMA, VENEZUELA, GUYANA, SURINAM, French Guiana, COLOMBIA, ECUADOR, Galápagos Islands (Ecuador), PERU, BRAZIL, BOLIVIA, PARAGUAY, URUGUAY, ARGENTINA, CHILE, WESTERN SAMOA, TONGA, PACIFIC OCEAN, Falkland Islands (UK), South Ge (UK), SOUT

Coniferous Forest

The vast coniferous forest that stretches round the northern hemisphere is called the taiga. Evergreen trees such as spruce, pine, fir, and larch are able to grow there (see right). The boundary between the taiga and the tundra is known as the tree line.

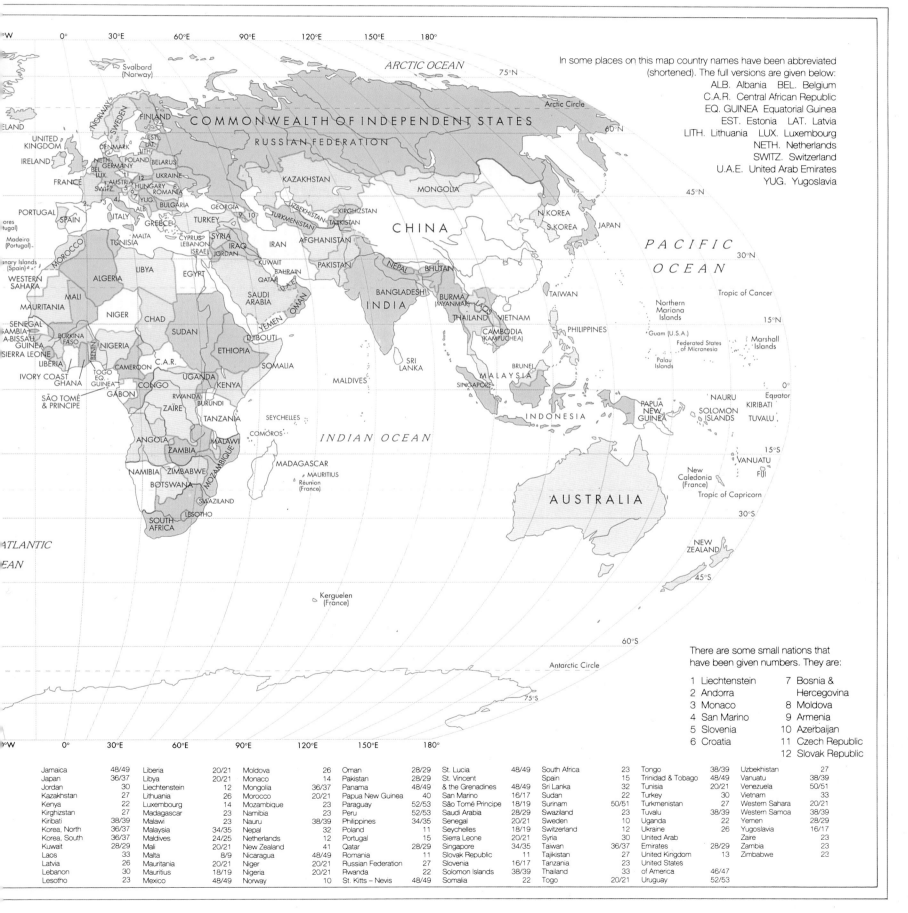

In some places on this map country names have been abbreviated (shortened). The full versions are given below:

ALB. Albania BEL. Belgium
C.A.R. Central African Republic
EQ. GUINEA Equatorial Guinea
EST. Estonia LAT. Latvia
LITH. Lithuania LUX. Luxembourg
NETH. Netherlands
SWITZ. Switzerland
U.A.E. United Arab Emirates
YUG. Yugoslavia

There are some small nations that have been given numbers. They are:

1	Liechtenstein	7	Bosnia &
2	Andorra		Hercegovina
3	Monaco	8	Moldova
4	San Marino	9	Armenia
5	Slovenia	10	Azerbaijan
6	Croatia	11	Czech Republic
		12	Slovak Republic

Jamaica	48/49	Liberia	20/21	Moldova	26	Oman	28/29	St. Lucia	48/49	South Africa	23	Tongo	38/39	Uzbekhistan	27
Japan	36/37	Libya	20/21	Monaco	14	Pakistan	28/29	St. Vincent		Spain	15	Trinidad & Tobago	48/49	Vanuatu	38/39
Jordan	30	Liechtenstein	12	Mongolia	36/37	Panama	48/49	& the Grenadines	48/49	Sri Lanka	32	Tunisia	20/21	Venezuela	50/51
Kazakhstan	27	Lithuania	26	Morocco	20/21	Papua New Guinea	40	San Marino	16/17	Sudan	22	Turkey	30	Vietnam	33
Kenya	22	Luxembourg	14	Mozambique	23	Paraguay	52/53	São Tomé Principe	18/19	Surinam	50/51	Turkmenistan	27	Western Sahara	20/21
Kirghizstan	27	Madagascar	23	Namibia	23	Peru	52/53	Saudi Arabia	28/29	Swaziland	23	Tuvalu	38/39	Western Samoa	38/39
Kiribati	38/39	Malawi	23	Nauru	38/39	Philippines	34/35	Senegal	20/21	Sweden	10	Uganda	22	Yemen	28/29
Korea, North	36/37	Malaysia	34/35	Nepal	32	Poland	11	Seychelles	18/19	Switzerland	12	Ukraine	26	Yugoslavia	16/17
Korea, South	36/37	Maldives	24/25	Netherlands	12	Portugal	15	Sierra Leone	20/21	Syria	30	United Arab		Zaire	23
Kuwait	28/29	Mali	20/21	New Zealand	41	Qatar	28/29	Singapore	34/35	Taiwan	36/37	Emirates	28/29	Zambia	23
Laos	33	Malta	8/9	Nicaragua	48/49	Romania	11	Slovak Republic	11	Tajikistan	27	United Kingdom	13	Zimbabwe	23
Latvia	26	Mauritania	20/21	Niger	20/21	Russian Federation	27	Slovenia	16/17	Tanzania	23	United States			
Lebanon	30	Mauritius	18/19	Nigeria	20/21	Rwanda	22	Solomon Islands	38/39	Thailand	33	of America	46/47		
Lesotho	23	Mexico	48/49	Norway	10	St. Kitts – Nevis	48/49	Somalia	22	Togo	20/21	Uruguay	52/53		

Europe is the smallest continent of the northern hemisphere. The Ural Mountains form a boundary with Asia to the east, and on the other three sides it is surrounded by sea. The coastline is 50,000 miles long, so nowhere in western Europe is far from a port. This has encouraged fishing and provided a cheap and easy way of carrying goods from one place to another.

Europe has many natural advantages. It is rich in coal and iron, there is a temperate climate, and a greater proportion of the land can be farmed than in any other continent.

A Cosmopolitan Society
Europeans have diverse origins, so their coloring and appearance are varied. Nordic people are fair, while most Mediterraneans are dark. Immigrants from Africa, Asia, and other countries make up a cosmopolitan society.

Industrial Wealth
Much of Europe's wealth comes from factories and mines. Britain, northern France, Belgium, and Germany are the principal manufacturing centers. They depend on their deposits of iron, coal, oil, and natural gas.

Scale approximately 1:17,200,000

```
0     200    400    600 km
0    100    200    300 miles
```

Food for all Seasons

Although Europe is intensively farmed, it cannot produce enough food for its vast population.

Grain, sugar beet, and potatoes are the main crops in the north and east. Wetter regions to the west provide pasture for dairy cattle. The mild climate of the south produces vines, olives, and citrus fruit.

A Land of Trees

An enormous variety of tree species grow throughout Europe. Evergreen conifers include pine, spruce, and fir trees (see left), while broadleaved trees that shed their leaves in autumn include oak, beech, and chestnut (see below).

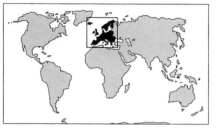

Facts and figures

Europe is a small continent, covering an area of 7.26 million sq.km. It extends from above the Arctic Circle to almost 34°N. There are no great mountain ranges or rivers to provide a dividing line between Europe and Asia. In this atlas, all of the former Soviet Union has been included in the Asian section. This also applies to Turkey which is half in Europe and half in Asia, spanning the Bosporus at Istanbul (see page 38).

There are nearly 500 million people living in Europe - more than in North America or Australasia. Only Asia has a larger population. Agriculture is important over much of Europe, and more than half the land is used for farming. Many farms use machines to cultivate the land and rely on the use of fertilizers and insecticides to produce more crops. However, these methods are causing concern because of the resulting chemical additives in food and because of the damaging effects of chemicals on the environment.

Most of Europe has a long history of industrialization. The Industrial Revolution started in Great Britain in the 1700s. Large manufacturing centres grew up. These were based around the supplies of coal and iron ore that were available. Large numbers of people moved into the towns to work.

The early development of many different manufacturing centres throughout the continent meant that there was an increase in the number of goods available for sale. This led to an increase in trade, which in turn led to an increase in wealth. Because of this, many Europeans have been able to enjoy a high standard of living.

Europe's Varied Wildlife
Much of the wildlife is threatened.

Population

The total population of Europe is about 500 million. The Vatican State has the smallest population at 1,000. The newly unified Germany has the largest with 77.45 million. The population density varies from virtually no people in some areas of northern Norway to over 400 per sq.km in the Netherlands.

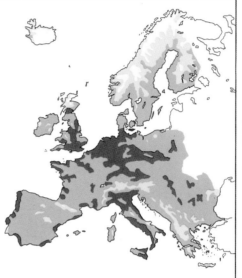

Number of people per square kilometre

■ >100	▨ 2-10
▨ 10-100	□ <2

Natural vegetation

So much of Europe's natural vegetation has been changed by human activities that most of the natural landscape has been lost. Large areas of forest have been cut down and much of the grassland has been built on or ploughed up as farmland.

□ Tundra/Mountain	▨ Mixed/Broadleaf Forest
□ Northern Forest	▨ Scrub

Climate

Because of the warm Gulf Stream, an ocean current that flows across the Atlantic and northwards past Great Britain, much of Europe's climate is mild. Generally temperatures are higher in Europe than in places with the same latitude in Asia and North America.

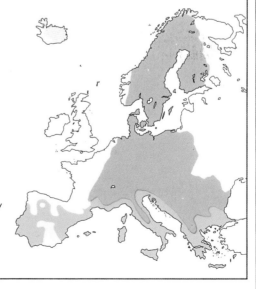

□ Arctic/Subpolar	▨ Subtropical – wet and dry
□ Oceanic/Maritime	□ Arid
▨ Continental	

Temperate Grasslands

Fertile meadows and woodland (see below) make up the North European Plain from England to Finland.

Arctic Tundra

Only a few hardy plants, such as the Arctic mouse ear below, survive the harsh conditions of the tundra.

Norway – Land of Conifers

In Norway, the coniferous forests of pine and spruce trees (see below) that cover a quarter of the land, are home to many birds (see above). Paper mills are situated at the mouths of rivers so that logs can be floated down to them and the products exported by sea.

F A C T   C H A R T

● In 1963 a volcanic eruption in the sea created a new island, Surtsey, off the south coast of Iceland. Ten years later the nearby island of Heimaey had to be evacuated when a volcano erupted and destroyed a town.

● Hammerfest in Norway is the world's northernmost town. From May to August the sun never sets, and from November to February it is dark all day.

● Glittertind (8,103 feet) in Norway is the highest mountain.

● Sweden's natural resources of water power, timber, and iron ore have made it one of the richest countries in the world.

● Lake Vänern (2,155 sq. miles) in Sweden is the largest lake in Scandinavia.

● Nearly a tenth of Finland consists of lakes. Raft-like ferries link the shores, but in winter the lakes freeze over and motorists drive over the ice.

● Denmark consists of the Jutland Peninsula and over 400 islands.

Scale approximately 1:8,333,000
At the scale of this map the straight line distance from Helsinki (D4) to Göteborg (B4) is approximately 494 miles (795 km).

The Scandinavian countries are Denmark, Sweden, Norway, Finland, and Iceland. Denmark is a small, flat, agricultural country with a dense population. Sweden and Finland consist largely of lakes and forests. Norway is a bare mountainous country with a long coastline. These last three have the lowest populations in Europe. Iceland is an island just south of the Arctic Circle.

Iceland – Land of Glaciers

Over a tenth of Iceland is covered by glaciers (see right). The largest is called Vatnajokull. At the same time, there is much volcanic activity.

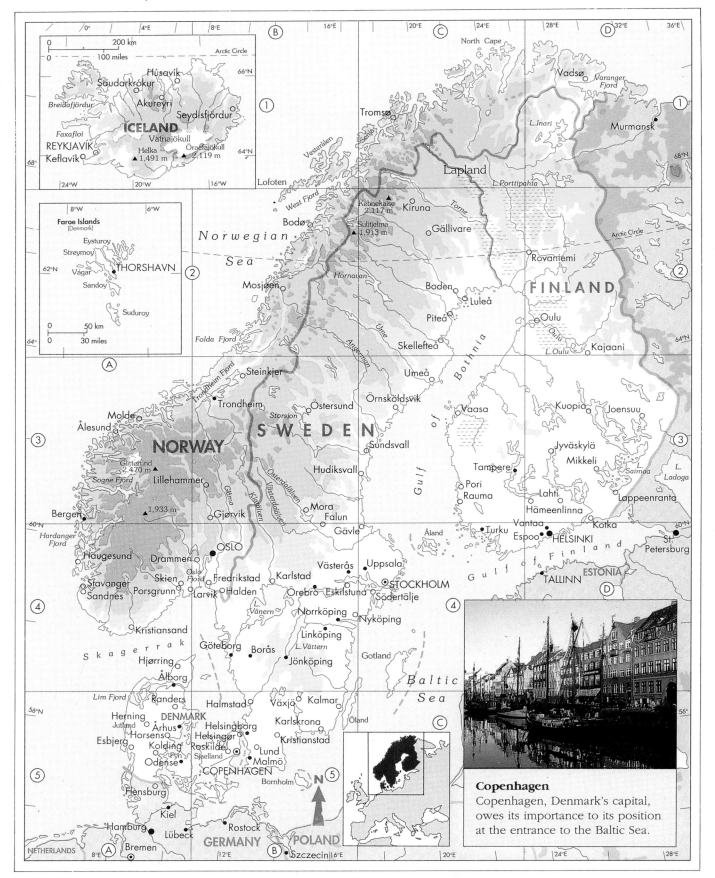

Copenhagen

Copenhagen, Denmark's capital, owes its importance to its position at the entrance to the Baltic Sea.

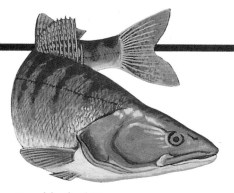

Land-locked Hungary
Hungary has no coastline, but the Tisza and Danube Rivers cross the Great Hungarian Plain and provide plenty of freshwater fish for food and sport.

Romania
The Black Sea (see right) has fine beaches and the summers are warm. It is a favorite holiday area.

Scale approximately 1:6,667,000
At the scale of this map the straight line distance from Gdansk (C1) to Bucharest (E4) is approximately 761 miles (1,226 km).

Eastern Europe is an area of contrasts. Poland is part of the North European Plain. The land is mainly agricultural. Austria and Romania are mountainous; the Czech and Slovak Republics are a mixture of fertile plains and high mountains. Hungary has low hills in the north, but is dominated by the vast Great Hungarian Plain where herds of horses roam. The climate is cold in winter and warm in summer.

The Historic Cities of Poland
Many towns in Poland, such as Warsaw (see above), were ruined in World War 2. Many have now been restored to their former glory.

FACT CHART

● Austria is one of Europe's most mountainous countries. Ranges and spurs of the Alps cover about 70 percent of the country.

● On January 1st 1993 Czechoslovakia split into two. The Czech Republic is in the west and the Slovak Republic is in the east.

● Lake Balaton in northwest Hungary is a favorite holiday resort. It covers an area of 245 square miles.

● Poland is one of the world's largest producers of meat, and the third largest producer of coal.

● Ploesti is the center of the Romanian oil industry. Romania is self-sufficient in oil and exports its surplus.

Austria – a Center of Culture
Vienna, the capital city of Austria, is one of the great cultural centers of Europe.

CENTRAL EUROPE

Germany, the wealthiest country in Europe, extends across much of Central Europe. The north, a low, flat plain, rises in the south towards the Alps. Belgium and the Netherlands are both small, flat countries. Much of the Netherlands is below sea level. The Dutch have built huge dykes to keep out the sea and drained large areas for farming. Switzerland and Liechtenstein, by contrast, are mountainous.

The Netherlands
The Dutch port of Rotterdam is the largest in the world. With over 75 miles of quayside, it is one of the busiest ports in Europe.

Swiss Alps
The Swiss Alps are popular with tourists for their flowers and skiing. Mountains cover 70 percent of the land.

The Center of the EC
The headquarters of the European Community are in Brussels. Belgium was one of the first six countries to found the EC in 1957.

FACT CHART

● In the last 800 years the Netherlands has lost about 14 million acres of land to the sea and reclaimed at least 17 million acres.

● The world's longest road tunnel, St Gotthard (over 10 miles), runs under the Alps in Switzerland.

● In Belgium the Flemings, who speak Flemish, live in the north. The French-speaking Walloons live in the south.

● The River Rhine in Germany, over 620 miles long, carries more shipping than any other river in the world.

● Liechtenstein, one of the smallest countries in the world at 62 square miles, has a population of 25,000.

Scale approximately 1:5,000,000
At the scale of this map the straight line distance from Geneva (B5) to Rostock (C2) is approximately 605 miles (974 km).

```
0        100        200 km
0     50        100 miles
```

German Castles
The River Rhine is famous for its ancient castles (see above). It has been an important trading route for centuries.

BRITISH ISLES

T he British Isles consist of Britain, Ireland and some small islands near their coasts. Britain contains England,

English Woodlands
Much of England was once covered by forests of trees such as the oak (see left). Most of these were felled for farm and building land.

Scotland, and Wales. Ireland is divided into Northern Ireland, which is part of the United Kingdom, and Ireland (Eire).

The landscape is very varied. Wales and Scotland have ranges of low mountains. But except for the Pennines, England is low-lying.

The Emerald Isle
Ireland was once part of the United Kingdom, but in 1922 it became an independent republic. The six counties of Northern Ireland (Ulster) stayed with the United Kingdom. The shamrock (see above) is the national emblem of Ireland.

Welsh Castles
Wales was divided into several small independent kingdoms until Edward I conquered the Welsh in the 13th century. Edward built several castles which still survive (see above). The Welsh language is taught in the schools and spoken by many people.

FACT CHART

● London is the largest city in Europe. It extends over an area of 630 square miles, and has about 8 million inhabitants.

● Nowhere in the United Kingdom is further than 70 miles from the sea.

● Scotland consists of a mainland and about 780 islands, many of which are uninhabited.

● The longest river in Ireland, the Shannon is 238 miles long.

● The highest point in Ireland is Carrantuohill (3,412 feet) in the southwest.

● The highest peak in Wales (3,600 feet) is in Snowdonia.

Scale approximately 1:5,250,000
At the scale of this map the straight line distance from Plymouth (C5) to Lerwick (C1) is approximately 684 miles (1,101 km).

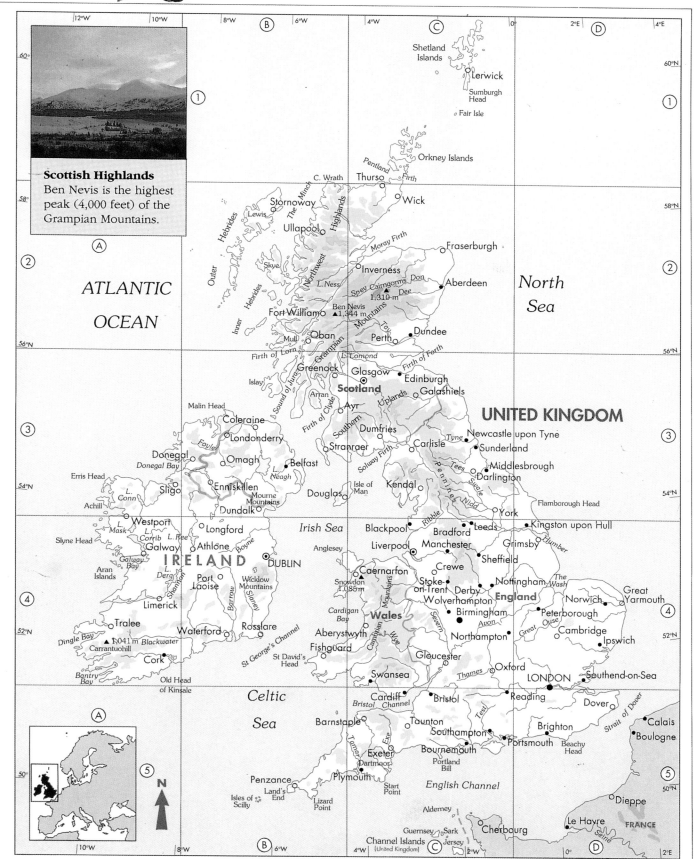

Scottish Highlands
Ben Nevis is the highest peak (4,000 feet) of the Grampian Mountains.

FRANCE

Wine and Cheese
Food is a major industry, over 250 French wines and 240 French cheeses are made (see above). The largest vineyard on earth (2,000,000 acres) is in southern France.

Scale approximately 1:5,555,000
At the scale of this map the straight line distance from Marseilles (D4) to Brest (A2) is approximately 592 miles (935 km).

```
0        100        200 km
0     50        100 miles
```

France, the second largest country in Europe, stretches almost 620 miles from north to south and from east to west. Almost a third of the land is cultivated and at least 25 percent of this is pasture. One-fifth of exports come from farm goods. Large supplies of coal, iron ore, bauxite (aluminum ore), sulfur, and natural gas have fueled a thriving industrial economy. With modern factories and the latest technology, France is among the top five industrial exporters.

Paris
The historic center of Paris is a major tourist attraction. Many people visit the famous Champs-Elysées and Arc de Triomphe (see right).

Luxembourg is a land of farms and forests with huge deposits of iron ore in the northeast. The small country of Monaco consists of two towns – Monaco and Monte Carlo.

FACT CHART

● France, the second largest country in Europe, has a highly developed transport system. Extensive highways, inland railways, and waterways enable rapid transport of people and goods across Europe.

● There are 22 regions in France, each with a Regional Council elected by the local people. Each region is divided into departments – there are 95 in all.

● France is a multiparty democracy. The French Parliament consists of two sets of elected members – the senate which has little legislative power (319 members) and the National Assembly, the principle law-making body (577 members). The elected President, who appoints the Prime Minister, resides at the Elysée Palace.

● Luxembourg, established in 963, is one of the oldest independent countries.

● Monaco is tiny – only 0.6 square miles.

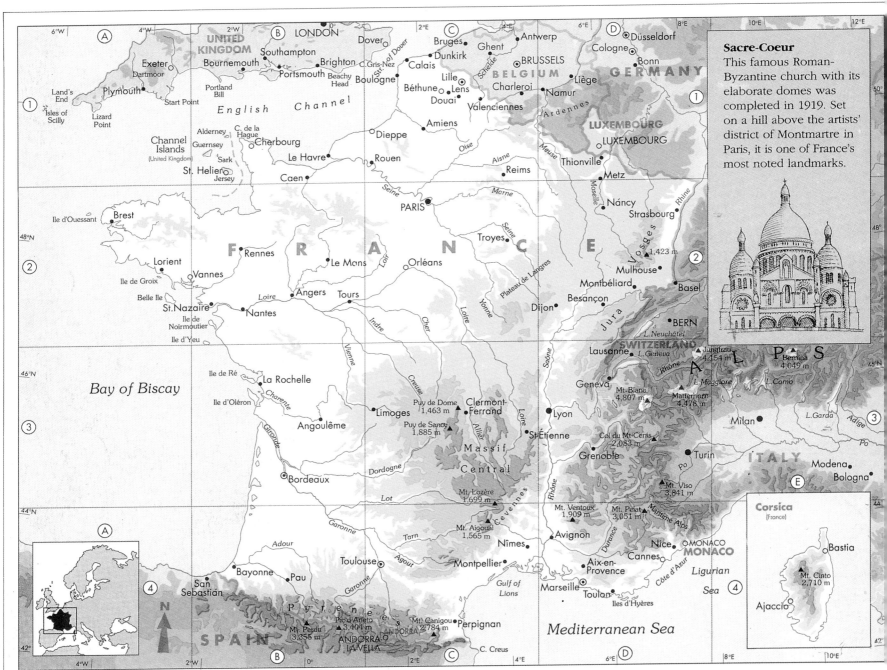

Sacre-Coeur
This famous Roman-Byzantine church with its elaborate domes was completed in 1919. Set on a hill above the artists' district of Montmartre in Paris, it is one of France's most noted landmarks.

SPAIN and PORTUGAL

FACT CHART

● Spain is the third largest country in Europe. Portugal lies on the west coast of Spain, bordering the Atlantic Ocean.

● Spain is a mountainous country, the chief mountain ranges being the Pyrenees, the Cantabrian Mountains, and the Sierra de Gredos. Spain's highest mountain, at over 11,200 feet, is the volcano Teide on Tenerife, the Canary Islands. Portugal's highest point, located in the Serra da Estrela, is 6,000 feet above sea level.

● Spain is among the top ten industrial countries in the world.

● Both Spain and Portugal are members of the EC.

Madrid

Madrid, the capital of Spain since 1561, is the seat of government and an industrial and communications center (see right).

Spain and Portugal occupy the Iberian Peninsula in southwest Europe. Spain includes two groups of islands – the Canaries and the Balearics.

Spain's economy is mostly based on services, including tourism, industry, and agriculture.

Large quantities of tomatoes, oranges, and wine are exported. Copper, lead, and zinc are mined in the Sierra Morena mountains, and reserves of iron and coal help fuel industry.

About 40 percent of Portugal is arable land and another 40 percent is covered by forests and woods. There is a mixed economy based on light and heavy engineering, particularly ship building and repair, and agriculture – wine, figs, and cork are all exported.

Scale approximately 1:5,000,000
At the scale of this map the straight line distance from Lisbon (A3) to Barcelona (E2) is approximately 623 miles (1,009 km).

Holy Week
Spain is renowned for its festivals such as Holy Week – the week before Easter (see above).

Hilltop Castles
The medieval castles of Spain and Portugal (see below) reflect their historic past.

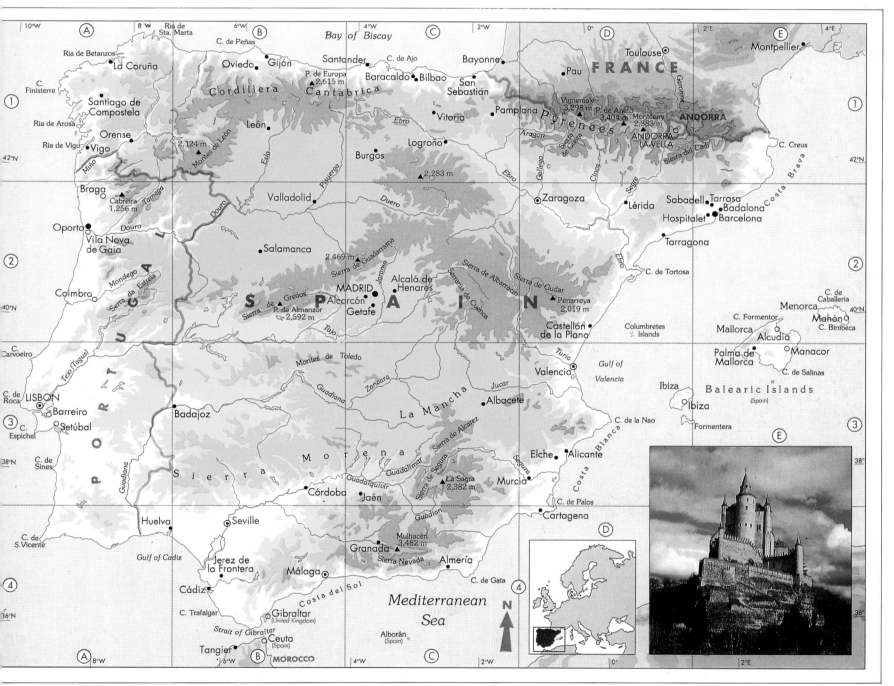

Yugoslavia
Belgrade (see above), the capital of Yugoslavia, is situated at the gateway from the Balkans to Central Europe. In April 1992, three former Yugoslavian states became independent countries – Croatia, Slovenia, and Bosnia and Hercegovina.

Bulgaria
Sofia (see above) is Bulgaria's capital city, and is known for its educational and cultural facilities. It was badly damaged in World War 2 and much of it has been rebuilt.

Wildlife
In some of the wilder areas of the region, wild boar (see above), wolves, wild goats, and ibex can be found.

Southern Europe consists of three great peninsulas: the Iberian Peninsula (Spain and Portugal), Italy, and the Balkan Peninsula. The Balkans (the Turkish word for mountains) includes Albania, Bulgaria, mainland Greece, European Turkey, parts of Croatia, Slovenia, Bosnia and Hercegovina, and Yugoslavia.

Some of these countries are the poorest in Europe, depending mostly on farming, although the conditions are not favorable. The climate is hot and dry, and the land mountainous. Fruit is a main crop and wheat and barley grow during the winter and ripen in early summer. Many people make a living from fishing. Yugoslavia has many resources including coal, lead, zinc, and copper.

Good beaches and plenty of sunshine have made many areas popular with tourists.

Italian Wheatfields
The Italians eat much bread and pasta. Wheat is an important crop on the northern plains, and in Apulia and Sicily.

Lands of Vines
Grapes are grown all over Italy and Greece. Each region produces its own type of wine.

Mediterranean Fruits
Greece is a leading exporter of lemons. The climate is ideal for growing citrus fruits. Southern Italy and Sicily grow lemons, oranges, peaches, grapefruit, and olives.

The Pantheon
The Pantheon (see below) is one of the sights of Rome. Many Ancient Roman buildings still survive in Italy.

FACT CHART

● Vesuvius, above the Bay of Naples, is the only active volcano on the European mainland.

● Greece has 166 inhabited islands. The largest of these is Crete. There are also 1,259 uninhabited ones.

● Slovenia's highest peak, Triglav, is 9,396 feet.

● Bulgaria is famous for its red roses, which grow in the valley of Kazanlyk, sheltered by the slopes of the Balkans.

● Albania is known locally as Shqiperi, which means "eagles' country" – an apt name for such a remote, mountainous land.

● Italy's longest river is the Po (418 miles); its largest lake is Lake Garda (143 sq. miles).

Scale approximately 1:5,882,000
At the scale of this map the straight line distance from Athens (F4) to Turin (A2) is approximately 963 miles (1,550 km).

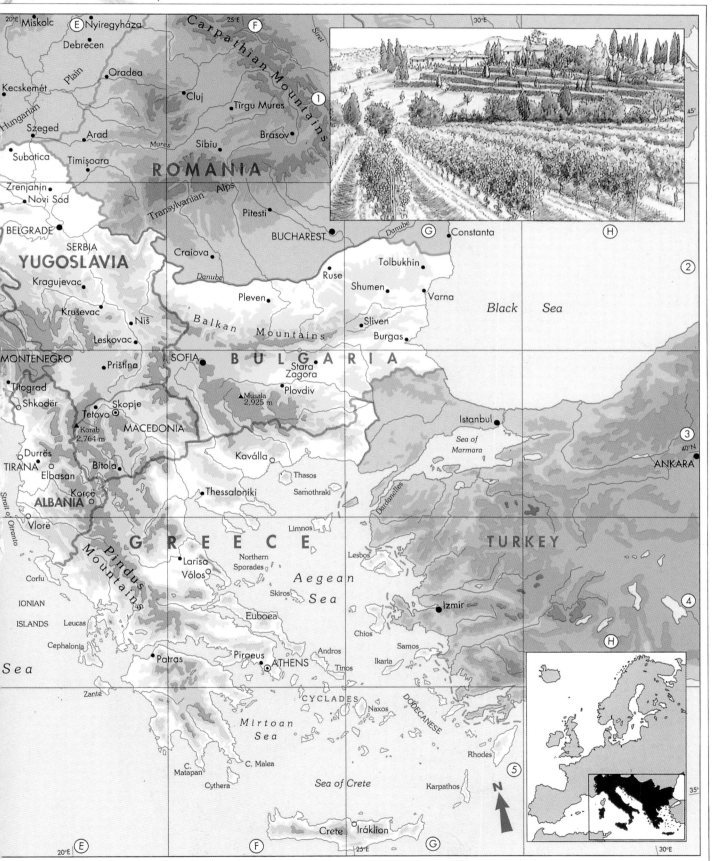

AFRICA

Rain Forests

Over 50 percent of Africa's natural rain forests (see below) have been cleared for timber and farming. Tree crops like cocoa, oil palm, and rubber grow well. Oil from the African oil palm (see above) is used to make margarine and soap.

Desert Sands

There are two main desert regions in Africa – the Sahara in the north and the Kalahari and Namib in the south. The plants that grow there, called succulents, store water in their roots, stems, or leaves (see below).

A frica, the warmest and second largest continent, extends almost 2,500 miles north and south of the Equator. It is a land of contrasts. Tropical rain forests grow around the Equator. These give way to huge plains of tropical grasslands that support herds of animals, especially in the wet season. Desert regions in the north and south have such low rainfall that few plants and animals can survive.

A few mountain ranges break up this vast plateau. The highest peaks, such as Mount Kenya and Kilimanjaro (Uhuru), are always covered in snow.

Population

Health care has improved greatly, especially for children, and this has led to a rapid increase in the total population. However, some areas cannot support large populations – of a total population of 670 million, almost 550 million live south of the Sahara. In the deserts, only fertile oases can support small settlements of people.

Number of people per square kilometer

- more than 100
- 10-100
- 2-10
- less than 2

Natural Vegetation

The natural vegetation and landscape of Africa are very diverse – from the hot Sahara desert to lush tropical jungle and from snow-topped mountain peaks to hot grassy plains. Much of the rain forest has been cut down, but some forests, such as the Korup National Park, are now protected areas.

- Tundra/Mountain
- Mixed Forest
- Scrub
- Grassland
- Tropical Rain Forest
- Tropical Forest
- Desert

Climate

Africa's climate is generally warm and hot because it lies between the tropics. The amount of rainfall varies greatly throughout the continent, and this determines the type of vegetation and climate. Some areas suffer from periods of drought, which has led to thousands of people dying from starvation.

- Subtropical - wet and dry
- Tropical - humid
- Tropical - wet and dry
- Arid

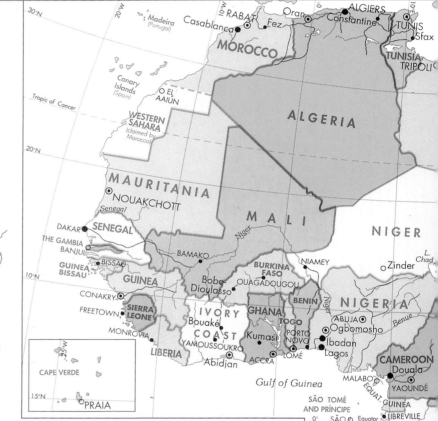

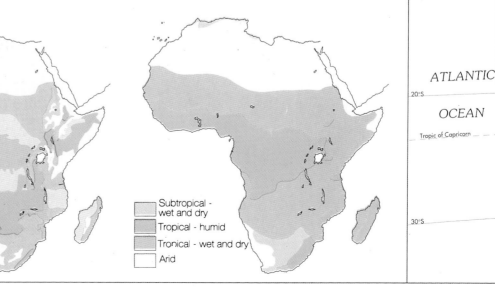

The Grasslands
The tropical grasslands, or savanna (see left), of Africa are home to lions, gazelles, zebras, and many other animals. Many of the plants, like the thorn trees, have long spines but this does not stop giraffes feeding on them (see right).

Health Care
Although medical advances have saved millions of lives, many children in Africa still die from childhood infections. Vaccination programs and effective health care are being introduced into many regions, such as here in Ethiopia (see below).

Food and Drink
Some vegetables, such as yams, are important staple foods in Africa. However, one local produce, coffee (see right), has spread throughout the world. It is now a widely cultivated plant prized for its seeds, which when dried and roasted make the commercial coffee bean.

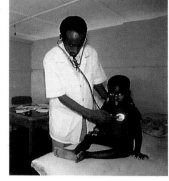

FACT CHART

● There are 52 independent countries in Africa, more than on any other continent. But most of them have fewer people than large cities such as London and Tokyo.

● Centuries ago, before Europeans colonized Africa, great empires flourished there. Some of their names, such as Benin and Zimbabwe, have been given to new, independent countries.

● Africa has vast deposits of copper, diamonds, gold, and oil. Some of the oldest known mines, in Swaziland, were mined for iron 43,000 years ago.

● The largest desert in the world, the Sahara, also has the highest sand dunes in the world – over 1,300 feet high and up to 3 miles long! However, only 30 percent of the Sahara is sand, the rest is rocky wasteland. It is also the sunniest place, with an average of 4,300 hours of sunshine a year.

● The longest river in the world, the Nile (4,135 miles) flows through North Africa to the Mediterranean Sea.

Scale approximately 1:32,000,000

| 0 | 500 | 1,000 km |
| 0 | 300 | 600 miles |

Map labels:

Mediterranean Sea
Misurata • Benghazi
Alexandria
CAIRO
Giza
Nile
Red Sea
Tropic of Cancer
LIBYA
EGYPT
CHAD
N'DJAMÉNA
Port Sudan
Omdurman • KHARTOUM
SUDAN
White Nile
Blue Nile
DJIBOUTI • DJIBOUTI
Dire Dawa • Hargeysa
ADDIS ABABA
ETHIOPIA
SOMALIA
Sarh
CENTRAL AFRICAN REPUBLIC
BANGUI • Bambari
Uele
L. Turkana
UGANDA
KAMPALA
KENYA
Kisumu
Shebelle
MOGADISHU
CONGO
Ubangi
ZAÏRE
RWANDA
Kismaayo
L. Victoria
KIGALI • Mwanza
NAIROBI
Kasai
BRAZZAVILLE
KINSHASA
Lualaba
BUJUMBURA
BURUNDI
Mombasa
Mbuji-Mayi
L. Tanganyika
DODOMA • Zanzibar
TANZANIA
Dar es Salaam
INDIAN OCEAN
Equator 0°
SEYCHELLES
VICTORIA
10°N
ANGOLA
Lubumbashi
L. Nyasa
COMOROS • MORONI
Mayotte (France)
Ndola
MALAWI
LILONGWE
Zambezi
ZAMBIA
Nampula
LUSAKA
Blantyre
MOZAMBIQUE
MADAGASCAR
Mozambique Channel
10°S
Zambezi
HARARE
ZIMBABWE
Beira
ANTANANARIVO • Toamasina
NAMIBIA
BOTSWANA
Bulawayo
MAURITIUS
PORT LOUIS
WINDHOEK
Serowe
Reunion (France)
Walvis Bay (South Africa)
Limpopo
GABORONE
PRETORIA
Tropic of Capricorn
20°S
MAPUTO
Johannesburg
MBABANE
SWAZILAND
Vaal
Bloemfontein
MASERU
LESOTHO
Orange
Durban
SOUTH AFRICA
Cape Town
Port Elizabeth
30°S
30°E 40°E 50°E

NORTH and WEST AFRICA

A land of contrasts, North Africa ranges from the warm plains of Morocco, where olives, vineyards, and citrus groves flourish, to the Atlas Mountains and the biggest desert in the world – the Sahara. The central plains are mostly grasslands, where the people farm their own plots of land and grow cash crops such as groundnuts.

Tropical forests border West Africa from the Gulf of Guinea inland. Many of these countries are watered by the mighty Niger. Wealthier than their neighbors, these lands are rich in tin, oil, bauxite, and diamonds.

Rain Forests
The lands close to the Equator are covered with dense rain forests. In West Africa they spread inland from the Gulf of Guinea. The hot, wet climate encourages growth of dense vegetation, which supports a huge variety of wildlife, like the bushbaby above.

Fruits of the Forests
The plant below, katemfe, is a natural sweetener. It is found in the tropical rain forests of West Africa. Used commercially, one-tenth of an ounce of katemfe extract makes 5 tons of sweetener.

Atlas Mountains

The Atlas Mountains (left) cross Morocco and extend across north Algeria into Tunisia. They are divided into three main regions. The Rif Atlas bordering the Mediterranean rises 8,000 feet above sea level. To the south is the Middle Atlas. Farther south still, the High Atlas contains Morocco's highest peak, Jebel Toubkal, at 13,665 feet.

Village Life

Many villages in Nigeria and Chad (see above) do not have running water. The people often wash their clothes and cooking pots in the river and lakes.

FACT CHART

● The River Niger flows for nearly 2,600 miles from its source in the southern highlands of Guinea into the Atlantic Ocean.

● Lake Chad is the remnant of an inland sea on the southern edge of the Sahara Desert. Four countries – Chad, Cameroon, Niger, and Nigeria – share the water, which is seldom more than 23 feet deep.

● In Ghana a great dam built across the River Volta has created a lake 250 miles long. The water is used to irrigate dry land and provide hydroelectric power.

● Libya has the largest oil reserves in Africa – the tenth largest in the world.

● Cave paintings of animals, including domestic cattle, suggest that the Sahara Desert was once wet enough to support plants and animals. Now the desert is expanding even further into Chad, Mali, and Senegal.

Scale approximately 1:15,957,000
At the scale of this map the straight line distance from Algiers (C1) to N'djamena (E4) is approximately 1,977 miles (3,183 km).

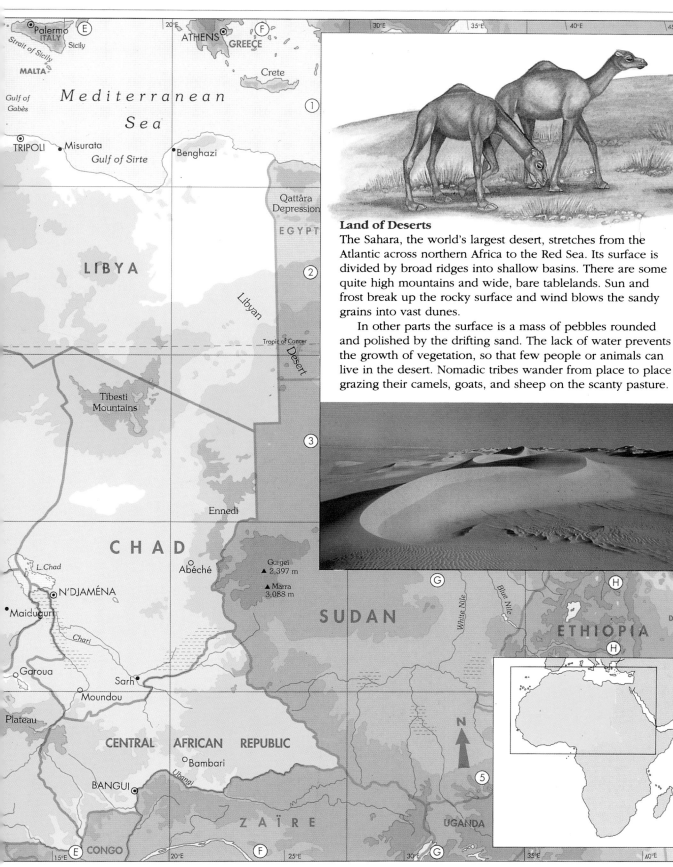

Land of Deserts

The Sahara, the world's largest desert, stretches from the Atlantic across northern Africa to the Red Sea. Its surface is divided by broad ridges into shallow basins. There are some quite high mountains and wide, bare tablelands. Sun and frost break up the rocky surface and wind blows the sandy grains into vast dunes.

In other parts the surface is a mass of pebbles rounded and polished by the drifting sand. The lack of water prevents the growth of vegetation, so that few people or animals can live in the desert. Nomadic tribes wander from place to place grazing their camels, goats, and sheep on the scanty pasture.

NILE VALLEY and EAST AFRICA

The Great Rift Valley – the largest crack in the Earth's crust – provides the most spectacular scenery in East Africa. In Kenya, the valley walls reach a height of 4,000 feet. The Eastern Rift ends at Lake Nyasa (Malawi); the Western Rift at Lake Tanganyika (4,710 feet deep).

The Nile delta is the most densely populated area. The wide plain is crossed by many channels and covered with fertile silt. Rice, cotton, and vegetables are grown. But beyond the range of the Nile floodwater, Egypt and Sudan are mostly desert.

The Masai People
The Masai travel in Kenya and Tanzania with their herds. The men become junior then senior warriors (see below).

Ancient Egypt
From early times people have lived in the fertile valley of the Nile. The golden mask of Tutankhamun (see above) from Luxor, and the pyramids and Sphinx (see below) near Cairo, are signs of one of the world's earliest civilizations.

FACT CHART

● Lake Assal in Djibouti is the lowest point in Africa at over 450 feet below sea level.

● The Aswan High Dam on the Nile is 2 miles long and 360 feet high. It has created a huge artificial lake, Lake Nasser, and greatly increased the area of irrigated land.

● Lake Victoria, Africa's largest lake and the second largest in the world, is 255 miles from north to south, and 155 miles broad. It stands at an altitude of 3,700 feet.

● The Red Sea, one of the saltiest in the world, separates Africa and Asia. It is long and narrow – about 1,200 miles from end-to-end and 125–250 miles broad.

Scale approximately 1:17,273,000
At the scale of this map the straight line distance from Cairo (B1) to Mombasa (C5) is approximately 2,409 miles (3,879 km).

```
0     250    500    750 km
|--|--|--|--|
0        200        400 miles
```

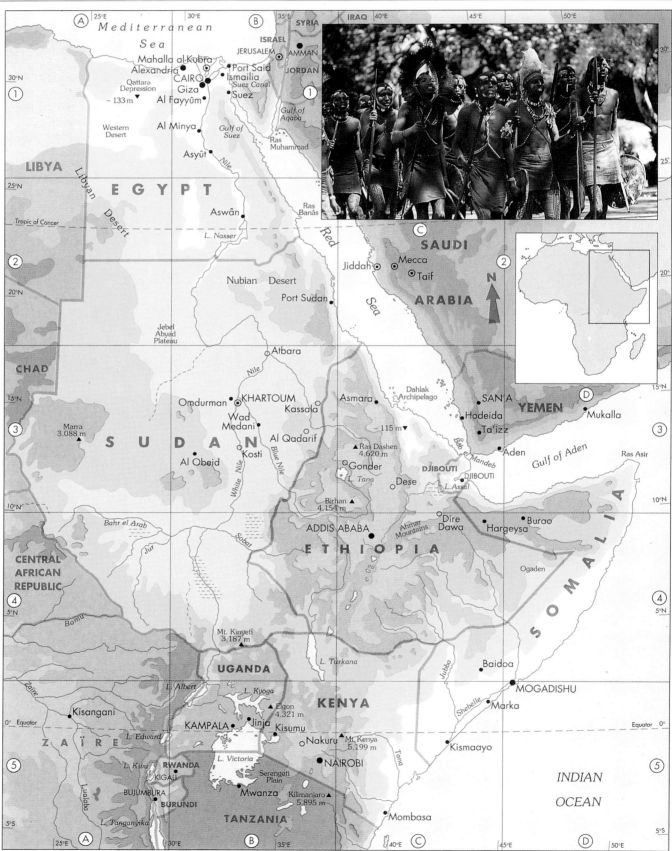

CENTRAL and SOUTH AFRICA

Animals of the African Plains
The grasslands of central Africa are home to many animals including antelopes, giraffes, zebras, and lions.

Central Africa has a tropical climate and much of it is covered in savanna grasslands. Many of the people depend on agriculture for their livelihood, but mining is also important.

South of the Zambezi the trees and tall grass give way to the dry, shrubby plains of the Kalahari Desert. In contrast, the open grassland, or veld, of South Africa is good farmland, rich in minerals.

Mining
Diamond mining is an important source of income in several African countries.

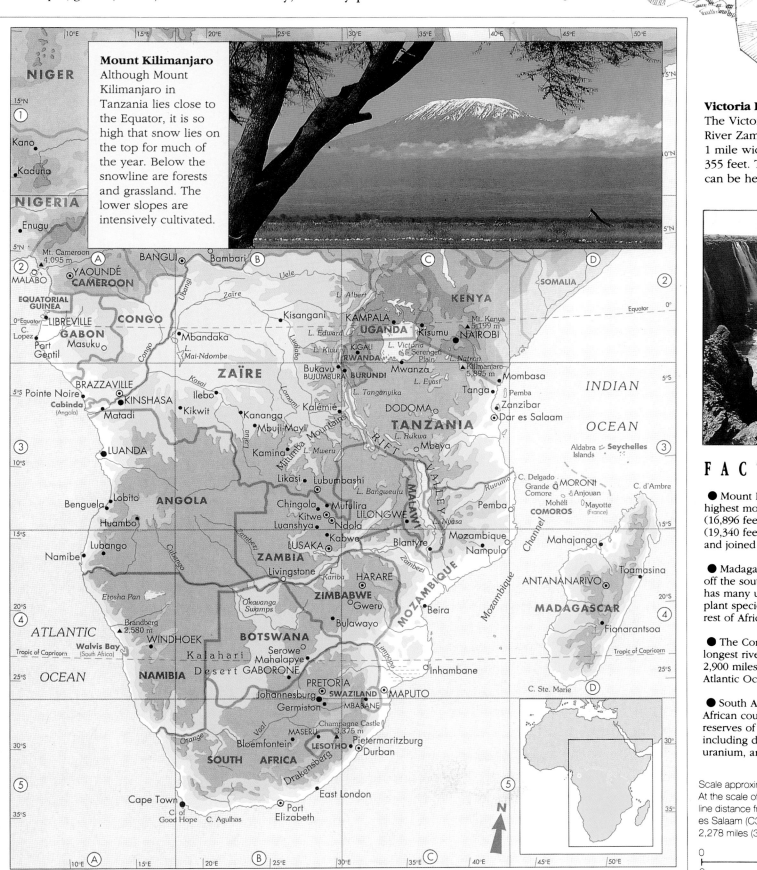

Mount Kilimanjaro
Although Mount Kilimanjaro in Tanzania lies close to the Equator, it is so high that snow lies on the top for much of the year. Below the snowline are forests and grassland. The lower slopes are intensively cultivated.

Victoria Falls
The Victoria Falls on the River Zambezi are over 1 mile wide and drop for 355 feet. The roar of water can be heard for 25 miles.

FACT CHART

● Mount Kilimanjaro is Africa's highest mountain. Kawenzi Peak (16,896 feet) and Kibo Peak (19,340 feet) are snow-capped and joined by a col, or pass.

● Madagascar, a large island off the southeast coast of Africa, has many unique animal and plant species not found in the rest of Africa.

● The Congo is the second longest river in Africa, flowing 2,900 miles from Zambia to the Atlantic Ocean.

● South Africa, the wealthiest African country, has large reserves of natural resources, including diamonds, gold, iron, uranium, and coal.

Scale approximately 1:25,330,000
At the scale of this map the straight line distance from Malabo (A2) to Dar es Salaam (C3) is approximately 2,278 miles (3,700 km).

```
0            500          1,000 km
0        300          600 miles
```

ASIA

Natural Resources
Northern parts of Asia are very rich in mineral resources. Gold, silver, diamonds, and other gemstones are all found in Siberia (see above).

Desert
Asia has both hot and cold deserts. The Thar Desert (see above) is swept by hot, dry winds that create vast sand dunes under the burning sun. The Gobi Desert of Mongolia and China is hot in summer, but the winters are long and bitterly cold.

Main Crops
Tea is a principal crop of India and southeast Asia. The tea bushes, grown in large plantations, are picked by hand, usually by women.

Asia is the world's largest continent – it occupies over one-third of the land surface. Stretching from the Arctic to the Equator and from the Urals to the Pacific Ocean, it is a land of great contrasts.

The climate ranges from some of the driest to the wettest, and the hottest to the coldest places in the world. The tundra of the extreme north gives way to the vast, unpeopled expanse of Siberia. Much of Asia is high – the central mountain ranges are the highest in the world. Their melting snows drain into the Indus, Ganges, Mekong, and Yangtze Rivers, providing water for the vast populations of India, China, and southeast Asia.

The Japanese islands, with the Philippines and Indonesia, ring the eastern part of Asia. This area is renowned for its many volcanoes and frequent earthquakes.

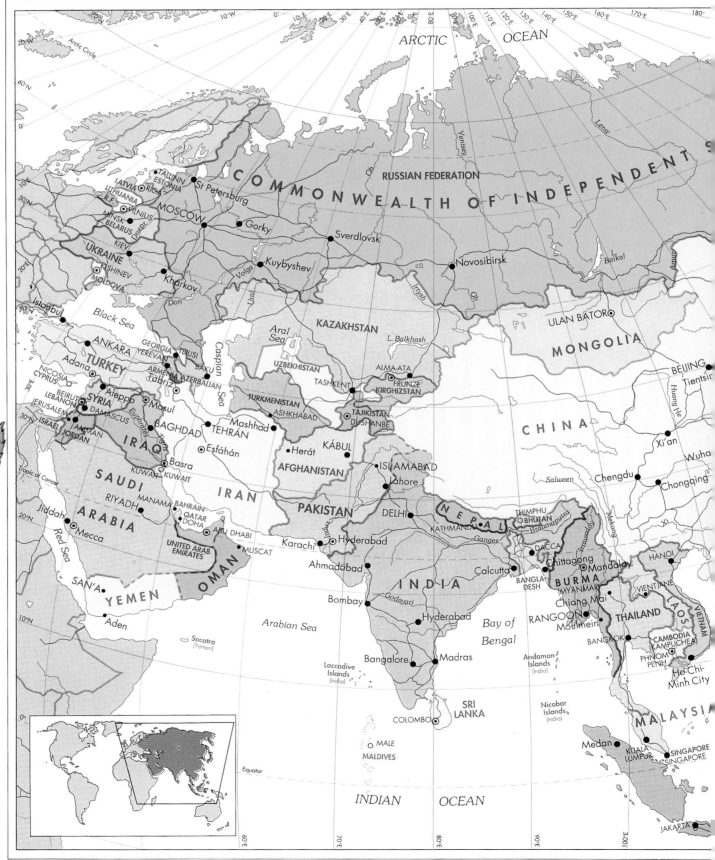

Scale approximately 1:40,000,000

0   500   1,000   1,500 km
0   300   600   900 miles

Farms and Farming
In many parts of Asia the people still use primitive farming methods. Oxen have been used for plowing for thousands of years (see left).

Family Life
Asians regard the family as very important. Grandparents, parent, aunts, uncles, and children often live together in an extended family (see below).

A Diet of Rice
Rice is the staple diet of half the world's population. It is an important crop in the hot parts of Asia where there is enough rain. The rice plants are grown in paddy fields standing in water. If the crop fails, there is often famine.

Population
Some parts of Asia are densely populated, whereas others have very few people living there. The southern and eastern lands are among the most crowded in the world. These lands are separated from northern Asia and Europe by barrier lands of deserts and high plateaus.

Number of people per square kilometer
- more than 100
- 10-100
- 2-10
- less than 2

Natural Vegetation
Asia's vegetation ranges from barren plains to coniferous forest and from grassy steppes to mountains cold deserts, and tropical forests.

- Tundra/Mountain
- Northern Forest
- Mixed/Broadleaf Forest
- Scrub
- Grassland
- Tropical Rain Forest
- Tropical Forest
- Desert

Climate
Asia's climate is variable. The Arctic and high central plateau are cold; the Thar Desert is hot and dry; Indonesia has two rainy seasons.

- Arctic/Subpolar
- Continental
- Subtropical – humid
- Subtropical – wet and dry
- Tropical – humid
- Tropical – wet and dry
- Arid
- High Altitude

FACT CHART

● Both the highest and lowest points on Earth are in Asia. Mount Everest is 29,028 feet at the highest peak. The shores of the Dead Sea are 1,309 feet below sea level.

● The largest lake in Asia is the Caspian Sea (about 143,000 sq. miles).

● The longest rivers in Asia are the Yangtze (3,500 miles), the Yenisey (3,400 miles), and the Huang He (3,395 miles).

● The Trans-Siberian Railway, which links Moscow with Vladivostok on the Pacific Ocean, is the longest railway line in the world. It is 5,800 miles long and the journey takes 7 days.

● Asia is the birthplace of all the major religions. Buddhism, Christianity, Confucianism, Islam, Hinduism, Judaism, Shinto, and Taoism all began in Asia.

● The main deserts of the region are the Gobi (500,000 sq. miles) and the Thar (74,000 sq. miles).

● The world's largest flower – Rafflesia – up to 3 feet across grows in the forests of Malaysia.

NORTHWEST ASIA

In December 1991 the Union of Soviet Socialist Republics (USSR) ceased to exist and the Commonwealth of Independent States (CIS) was founded by eleven former Soviet Republics. The three Baltic states of Estonia, Latvia, and Lithuania, and the former republic of Georgia have not joined the Commonwealth. It is an economic and political association of independent sovereign states.

Bounded by the Urals, northwest Asia is a land of forest and seas. The region is important for agriculture, timber, and oil as well as tourism.

National Dress
Distinctive traditional costumes, like these from Georgia, are worn on special occasions in many regions.

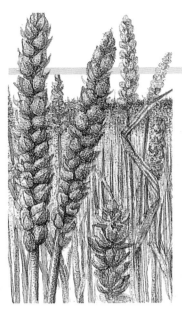

The Ukraine Steppes
The "black soil" lands of the Ukrainian steppes are one of the most important wheat-producing areas of the world.

Estonia
Tallinn (see above), the capital of Estonia, is famous for its song festivals featuring thousands of singers.

FACT CHART

● The Caspian Sea (139,230 sq. miles) is the world's largest inland body of water. It was once joined to both the Black Sea and the Aral Sea.

● The River Volga, popularly known as "Mother Volga", is 2,300 miles long.

● The Aral Sea – the fourth largest inland sea – is strewn with 1,300 tiny islands.

Baltic Wildlife
The mixed woodlands of the region are home to a variety of animals including lynx, badgers (see right), deer, and elk.

Scale approximately 1:18,000,000
At the scale of this map the straight line distance from Riga (A3) to Baku (C5) is approximately 1,623 miles (2,614 km).

| 0 | 250 | 500 | 750 km |
| 0 | 200 | | 400 miles |

NORTH and CENTRAL ASIA

St Basil's Cathedral, Moscow
St Basil's Cathedral in Moscow's Red Square (see above) is a reminder of the Byzantine culture and architecture of earlier times.

Famous Food
Caviar, a valuable export and one of the world's most expensive foods, is produced in the region of Kamchatka.

Siberia (Tatar for "sleeping land") covers most of North and Central Asia. The vast western Siberian plain, drained by the Ob and Yenisey rivers, is low-lying and swampy with coniferous forests. The central plateau rises to 5,580 feet in the Putoran Mountains and is drained by the Lena River. Eastern Siberia is mountainous, with areas of steppe and tundra. Siberia is notorious for its long, cold winters with temperatures as low as –89°F.

Siberian Plain
Siberia is rich in minerals, and there are many mining settlements. In winter (see above) the land is snow-covered.

FACT CHART

- Lake Baikal, 395 miles long, is the largest freshwater lake in Eurasia. At 5,700 feet deep it is the deepest lake in the world. It remains frozen for 4 months of the year.

- Over 350 rivers flow into Lake Baikal, but only one – the Angara – flows out.

- Verkoyansk and Omyyakon in northeast Siberia are the coldest inhabited places in the world with winter temperatures as low as –89°F.

Scale approximately 1:31,035,000
At the scale of this map the straight line distance from Omsk (B3) to Vladivostock (E3) is approximately 2,683 miles (4,320 km).

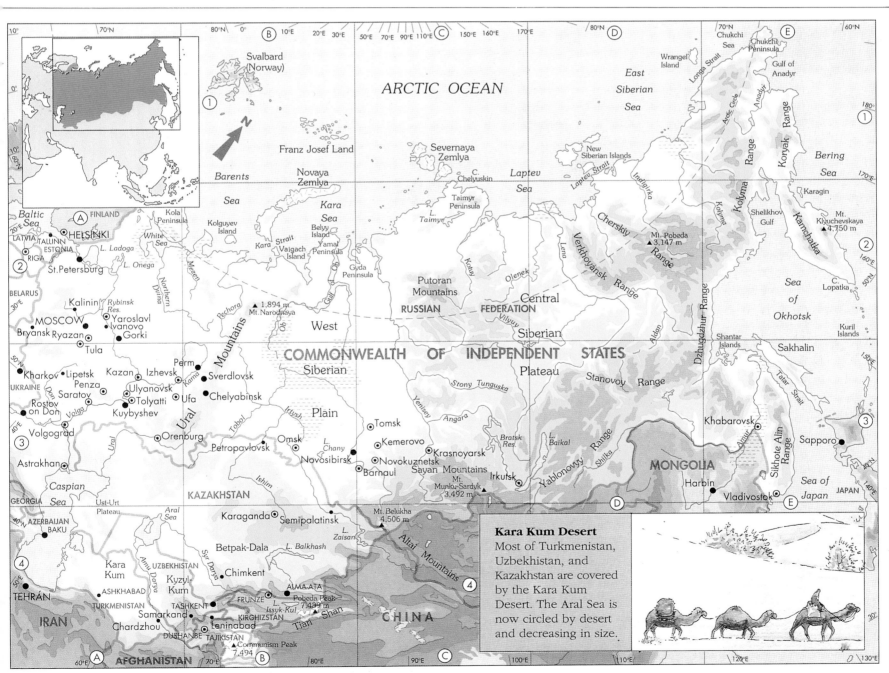

Kara Kum Desert
Most of Turkmenistan, Uzbekhistan, and Kazakhstan are covered by the Kara Kum Desert. The Aral Sea is now circled by desert and decreasing in size.

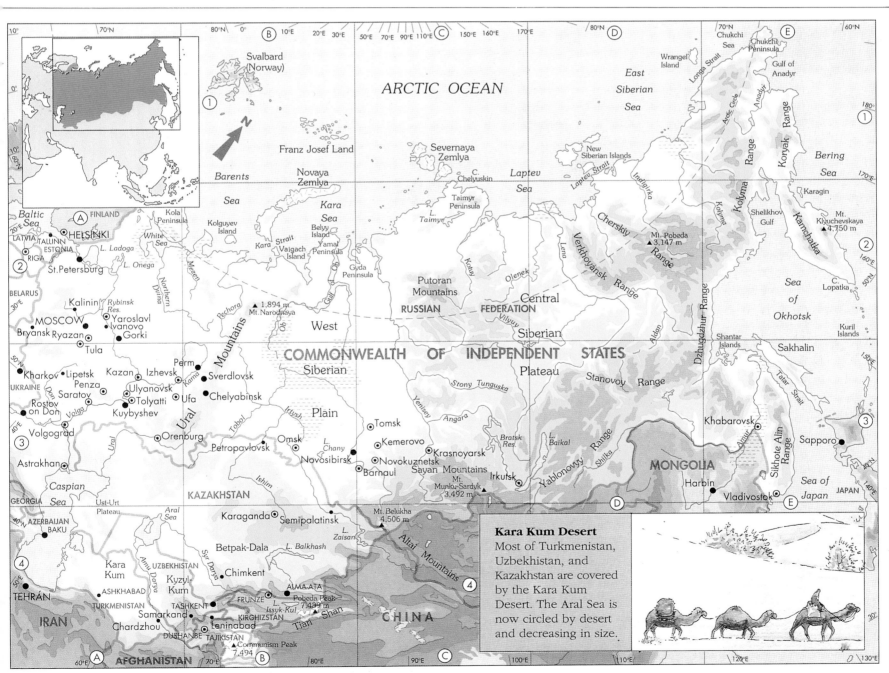

27

SOUTHWEST ASIA

Desert Wildlife
Dry scrub and desert cover vast regions. Most animals like these desert mice (see above) emerge at dusk to hunt and feed.

Muslim Religion
Islam is the religion of the Arab states. All Muslims pray five times a day, at a mosque if possible (see above).

FACT CHART

● The Pamirs, where China, India, Pakistan, and Afghanistan meet, are called the "Roof of the World." The mountains rise over 25,000 feet above sea level.

● K2, in the Karakoram Mountains, is the second highest peak in the world (28,250 feet high).

● The Khyber Pass, an important trading route between northwest Pakistan and the Kabul plain of Afghanistan, is little more than 600 feet wide for part of its length.

● The Euphrates and the Indus are the two great rivers of southwest Asia. Both of them are about 1,700 miles long.

● The United Arab Emirates (UAE), a federation of seven independent Arab states (Abu Dhabi, Dubai, Sharjah, Ras al Khaimah, Fujeira, Ajman, and Umm) is one of the richest countries in the world. Its wealth comes from oil.

Southwest Asia, which is sometimes called the Middle East, encompasses a variety of landscapes. They range from the sandy deserts of Saudi Arabia, to the mountains of the Hindu Kush, and the low-lying valley and wide delta of the River Indus in Pakistan.

Cultures and lifestyles vary greatly. Areas that lie within the "fertile crescent" between the Tigris and Euphrates are rich farmlands. The wealth of the Gulf countries comes from their oil. Afghanistan and Pakistan, poor countries with few resources, depend on agriculture.

Bedouin Camp
The Bedouins of the Arabian deserts are nomadic people. Many still live in tents woven from goat's hair.

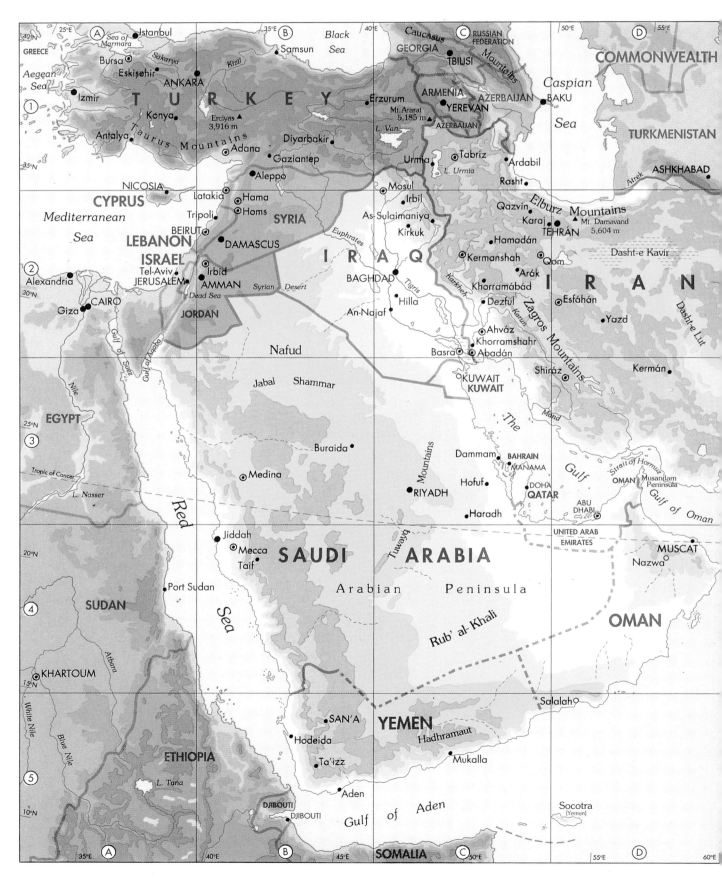

Arabian Markets

The Arabs are keen traders. Most towns have a market, or souk, where shoppers bargain for local wares. The stalls display a wide range of leather goods, brassware, pottery, jewellery, and colorful carpets. The people protect themselves from the burning sun by wearing loose clothes and headdresses (see right).

Houses for Hot Climates

These older houses in southern Iraq (see right) are very basic but are well suited to the hot climate. The flat roofs are used for drying crops or pottery in the sun. Families sometimes sleep out on the roof when the summer nights are very hot. The small windows help to keep the interior of the house cool in summer and warm in winter.

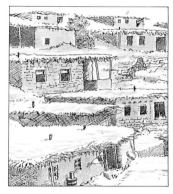

Ancient Skyscrapers

These buildings in Sana, in the Yemen, are more than 1,000 years old. They are built in the traditional mudbrick style, with shafts running up the center to take fresh air to each floor. The people live in extended families, so that a single building may house all the members of one family.

Family Wealth

The wealth of many Arabian families was stored as jewellery rather than money. This jewellery comes from Oman.

Scale approximately 1:15,000,000
At the scale of this map the straight line distance from Riyadh (C3) to Kabul (F2) is approximately 1,510 miles (2,431 km).

| 0 | 200 | 400 | 600 km |
| 0 | 100 | 200 | 300 miles |

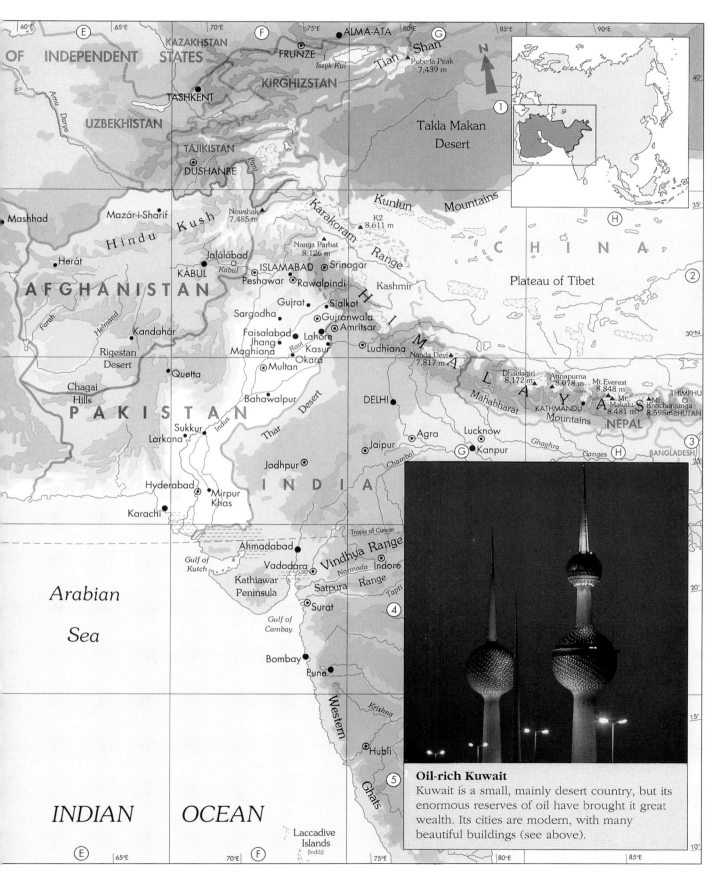

Oil-rich Kuwait

Kuwait is a small, mainly desert country, but its enormous reserves of oil have brought it great wealth. Its cities are modern, with many beautiful buildings (see above).

EASTERN MEDITERRANEAN

Offshore Oilrigs
The Gulf has numerous oilrigs (see above) and is dotted with terminals, loading platforms, and refineries.

The eastern Mediterranean Sea is bordered by Turkey, Syria, Lebanon, and Israel. The fertile coastal plains, where most people live, have a mild climate. Further inland the ground rises to a plateau of steppe and then merges into hot desert.

Turkey, which is separated into two by the Bosporus, is a land of farms, scrub, steppe, and pasture. Jordan, an inland country of mostly desert plateau, has few resources. Most people live in the more fertile west and north. The beautiful island of Cyprus, consisting of two

Ancient Cities
In the Eastern Mediterranean there are many remains of ancient cities such as Palmyra in Syria (see left).

mountain ranges with a broad plain between, lies in the northeast Mediterranean.

The Useful Date Palm
Date palms have been cultivated for hundreds of years, and every part of the tree is useful. Dates are one of the most important foods of the region. They are eaten fresh or dried.

FACT CHART

● The Dead Sea is the lowest point in the world – 1,300 feet *below* sea level. It is not really a sea at all, but a salt lake. It is five times as salty as the ocean.

● Agri Dagi – Mount Ararat – is the highest peak in Turkey (16,853 feet).

● Israel was founded after World War 2 as a home for the Jewish people. Over a million Jews from all over the world have settled there since 1948.

● The Bosporus, which means "ox ford" is a short narrow strait that separates Europe from Asia Minor. It is 18 miles long and less than half a mile wide at its narrowest point.

Scale approximately 1:7,895,000
At the scale of this map the straight line distance from Istanbul (A1) to Jerusalem (C3) is approximately 727 miles (1,170 km).

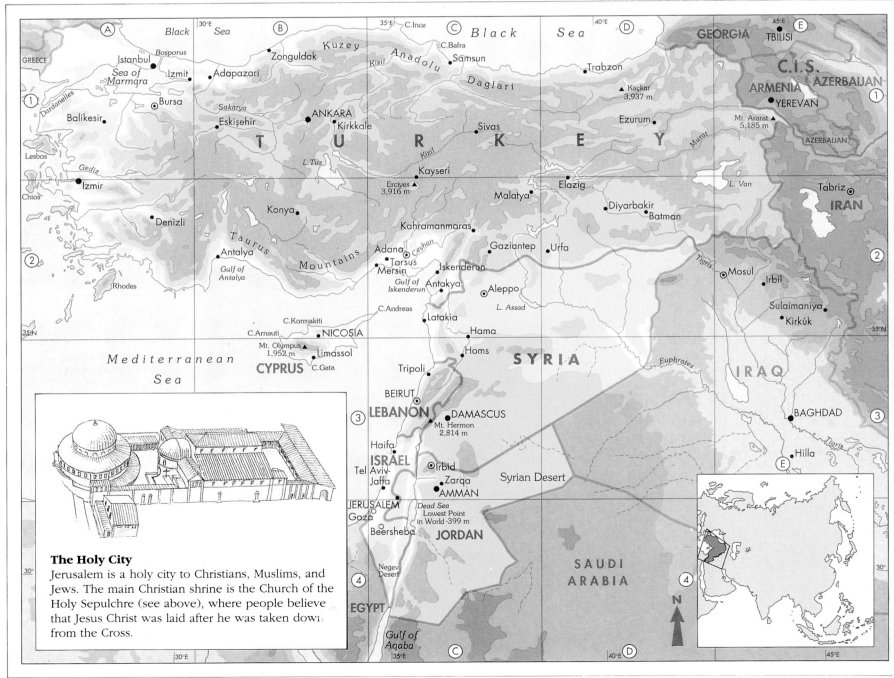

The Holy City
Jerusalem is a holy city to Christians, Muslims, and Jews. The main Christian shrine is the Church of the Holy Sepulchre (see above), where people believe that Jesus Christ was laid after he was taken down from the Cross.

THE GULF

FACT CHART

● The Ghawar oilfield in Saudi Arabia is the world's largest. It has twice as much oil as the entire reserves of the United States.

● In addition to the enormous reserves of oil, the Gulf region has nearly 25 percent of the world's natural gas reserves.

● Bahrain is a group of islands 20 miles off the east coast of the Gulf. The largest island is only 30 miles long and about 10 miles wide.

● The Middle East now produces about 10 million barrels of oil a day (one barrel is about 35 gallons).

Scale approximately 1:7,500,000
At the scale of this map the straight line distance from Kuwait (B2) to Abu Dhabi (D3) is approximately 520 miles (837 km).

0   100   200   300 km
0   50   100   150 miles

The Gulf is the arm of the Arabian Sea that lies between the deserts of Arabia and Iran. It is about 600 miles long and 200 miles wide, narrowing to 50 miles at the Strait of Hormuz, where it connects with the Gulf of Oman. The great rivers, the Tigris and the Euphrates, reach the Gulf at its northern end.

The Gulf is very shallow, with an average depth of only 330 feet. Its waters are warm, sometimes reaching 95°F in the summer. Once famous for its pearl-bearing oysters, its vast oil

reserves are now commercially much more important. The Gulf states derive their wealth from exporting oil to Europe, Japan, and North America.

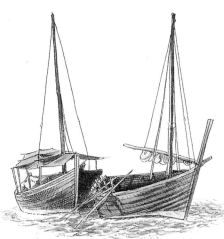

Local Fishing

Fish are an important resource in the Gulf. Commercial trawlers are usually used, but some of the local people still use the traditional *dhow* (see right).

Cool Clothes

Many people in the region wear loose-fitting robes and headdresses. They protect people from the sun and dust and keep them cool.

Istanbul

Istanbul (see below) is Turkey's chief port and center of trade. It lies on the shores of the Bosporus.

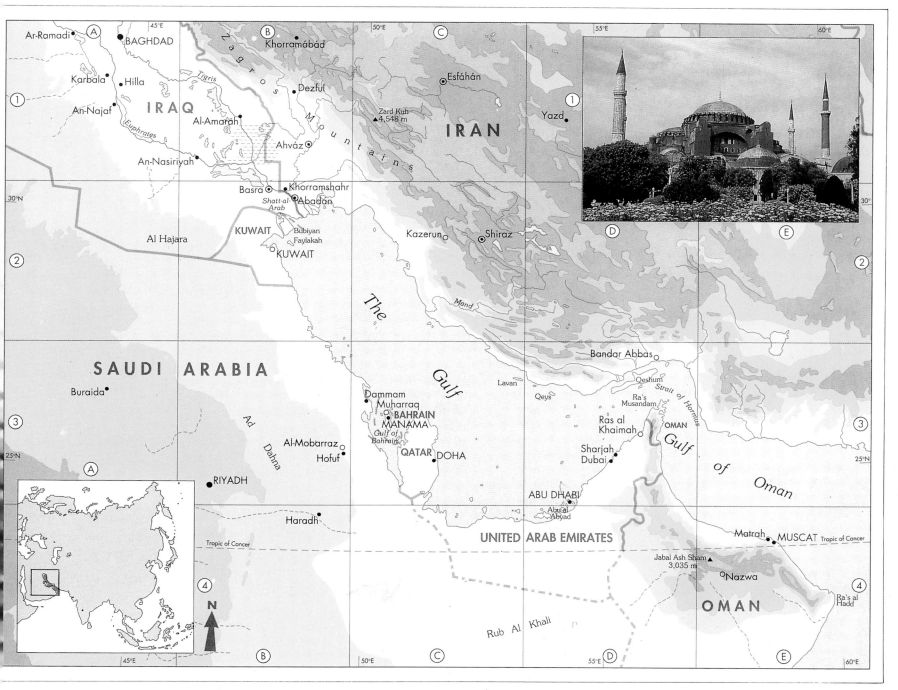

SOUTH ASIA

Over one billion people live in southern Asia. Most of them are farmers who live on the wetter coasts and in the fertile plains.

India, the largest country in South Asia, is a flat plateau, with mountain ranges on the east and west coasts and to the north.

The Thar Desert lies to the west Bangladesh, consisting of the flat, fertile floodplain of the Ganges, is dramatically affected by the annual monsoon.

Mount Everest

Mount Everest (see below) lies on Nepal's border with China. At 29,028 feet, it is the world's highest mountain.

Ancient Temples

The Hindu temples at Petua in northwest Bangladesh were built around 1,200 years ago.

The Lotus Flower

The pink-flowered lotus, a native to South Asia, is sacred to the Hindus.

Indian Tiger

Tigers are found in many areas of Asia. There are more Indian tigers (see above) than any other kind in the wild.

FACT CHART

● Around 871 million people live in India – 16 percent of the world's population.

● The Kingdom of Bhutan has a small population of about 1½ million. Only 9,000 people live in Thimphu, the capital.

● The Ganges, South Asia's longest river, rises in a Himalayan ice cave and flows 1,550 miles to the floodplain of Bangladesh.

● India has two monsoon winds – the southwest brings rain from June to September; the northeast blows from October to February.

● India has 25 main languages and more than 1,600 local languages.

Scale approximately 1:15,957,000
At the scale of this map the straight line distance from Kathmandu (C2) to Colombo (B5) is approximately 1,473 miles (2,372 km).

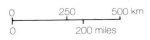

0   250   500 km
0   200 miles

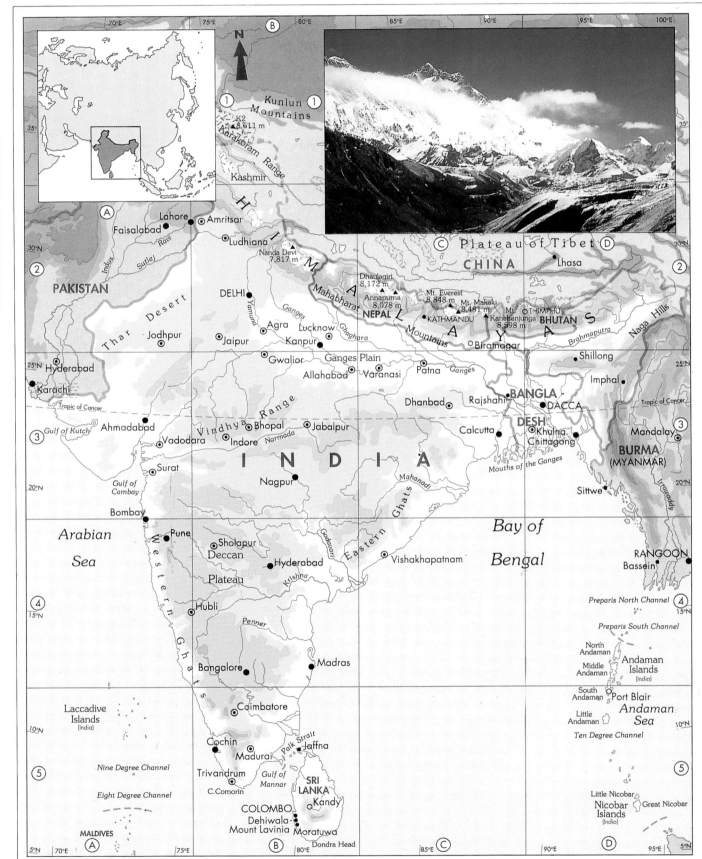

INDOCHINA

Tropical Fruit
The hot, wet climate is ideal for growing tropical fruits (see above).

The lands of Indochina – Burma (Myanmar), Thailand, Laos, Cambodia (Kampuchea), and Vietnam – are mountainous. Burma, bordered by mountains to the west, north, and east, has a tropical climate with evergreen rain forests, lush mangrove swamps, and monsoon forests.

The mountains of Thailand and Laos are thickly forested. Many of the people make their living from forestry. Cambodia and Vietnam are mainly agricultural.

Laos
The triumphal arch in Vientiane, the capital of Laos, is a famous landmark (see below).

Natural Resources
Some of the world's finest gemstones, including rubies, jade, and silver, are mined in the mountains of Burma.

Classical Dance
Classical dancers from Sri Lanka, Thailand (see above), and Indonesia train from childhood to perform the country's traditional stories. Dance dramas are frequently performed at Hindu and Buddhist festivals.

FACT CHART

● The Mekong is the major river of Indochina. It rises in the Tibetan mountains and flows southwards for 2,600 miles through Laos and Cambodia to southern Vietnam.

● Burma's highest peak is Mount Hkakabo at 19,578 feet above sea level.

● The River Irrawaddy flows for 1,300 miles through the heart of Burma. The delta is a vast paddy field nearly 200 miles wide.

● The Red and Mekong River deltas in Vietnam are less than 10 feet above sea level – they are the main farming areas.

● The Kohne Falls on the Mekong River in Laos are a series of rapids 6 miles long.

Scale approximately 1:11,538,500
At the scale of this map the straight line distance from Hanoi (C2) to Songkla (B5) is approximately 1,000 miles (1,610 km).

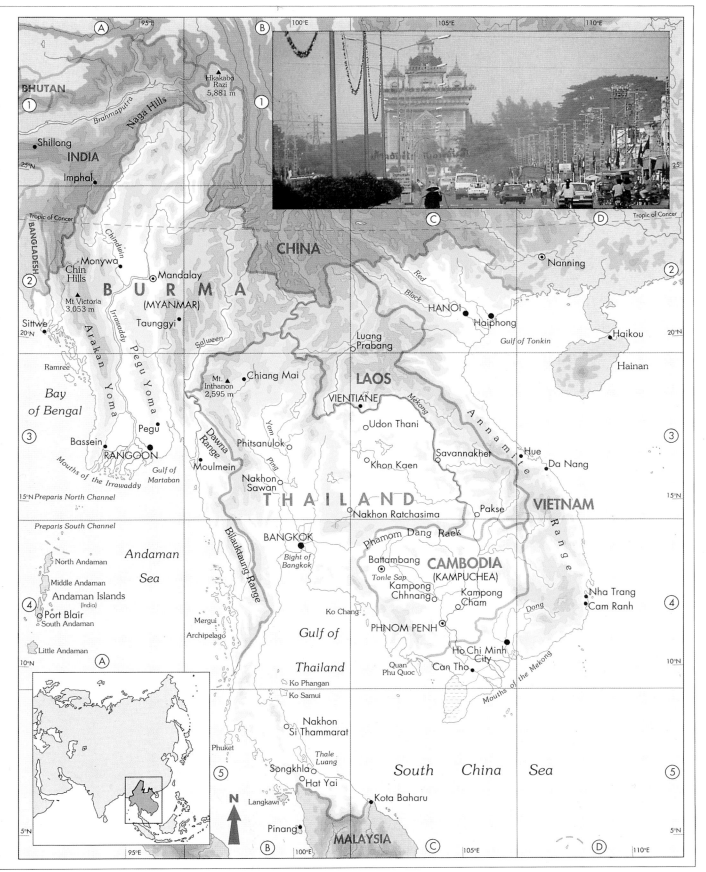

Southeast Asia is a complex mixture of modern trading nations and traditional farming communities. Its tropical rain forests and mangrove swamps are a haven for wildlife.

Malaysia has two distinct regions – 80 percent of the population lives on the Malay Peninsula and the rest in the states of Sarawak and Sabah, on the island of Borneo.

Indonesia is composed of hundreds of tropical islands in the Pacific and Indian Oceans. This vast area is subject to severe earthquakes and has many volcanoes.

The Spice Trade
Centuries ago, Arab merchants used to bring spices to Europe from the Moluccas, a large group of islands also known as The Spice Islands. Nutmeg, mace (see above), cinnamon, cloves, and pepper are still the traditional crops.

Kuala Lumpur
Kuala Lumpur (see above), the capital of Malaysia and the seat of government, is a mixture of ancient and modern buildings.

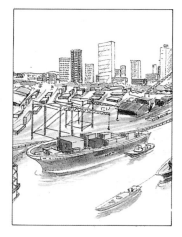

Singapore
Singapore is an important center for trade and finance, and one of the world's busiest ports (see above).

Scale approximately 1:13,636,000
At the scale of this map the straight line distance from Singapore (B3) to Balikpapan (D4) is approximately 915 miles (1,473 km).

```
0        200      400 km
0     100      200 miles
```

Disappearing Wildlife

Every year, vast areas of Asian forests are cut down for timber or cleared for farming. This means that natural habitats for numerous plants and animals like the giant hornbill (see left) and the orangutan of Borneo (see right) are being destroyed. Many of the local people who opposed the logging of the forests have lost their homes.

Houses on Stilts

In Southeast Asia houses are often built on stilts to protect them from floods caused by the monsoon. Along the coasts and around the islands whole fishing villages are built on stilts and can only be reached by boat. The houses are connected to each other by a series of floats (see left).

Terraces of Rice

In the Philippines, rice is still grown on terraces that have been in use for over 3,000 years. The supply of water is carefully controlled so that two or even three crops a year are possible (see left).

F A C T   C H A R T

● The highest peak in the Philippines is Mount Apo (9,692 feet); the largest lake is Laguna de Bay (356 sq. miles).

● Krakatoa, an island volcano between Sumatra and Java, exploded in 1883 in one of the greatest eruptions ever recorded.

● Singapore is one of the most densely populated places with almost 3 million people.

● Indonesia has over 13,600 islands and has more active volcanoes than anywhere else.

● Borneo is one of the hottest and wettest places in the world.

● Nearly 75 percent of tropical hardwoods come from Asia.

● As much as 5 feet of rain falls during the monsoon.

● Puncak Jaya (16,503 feet) in Irian Jaya is the highest peak.

● The Philippines has over 7,000 islands.

Brunei

Brunei lies on the north coast of the island of Borneo. The wealth produced from oil deposits means that most people have a high standard of living and food is plentiful (see above).

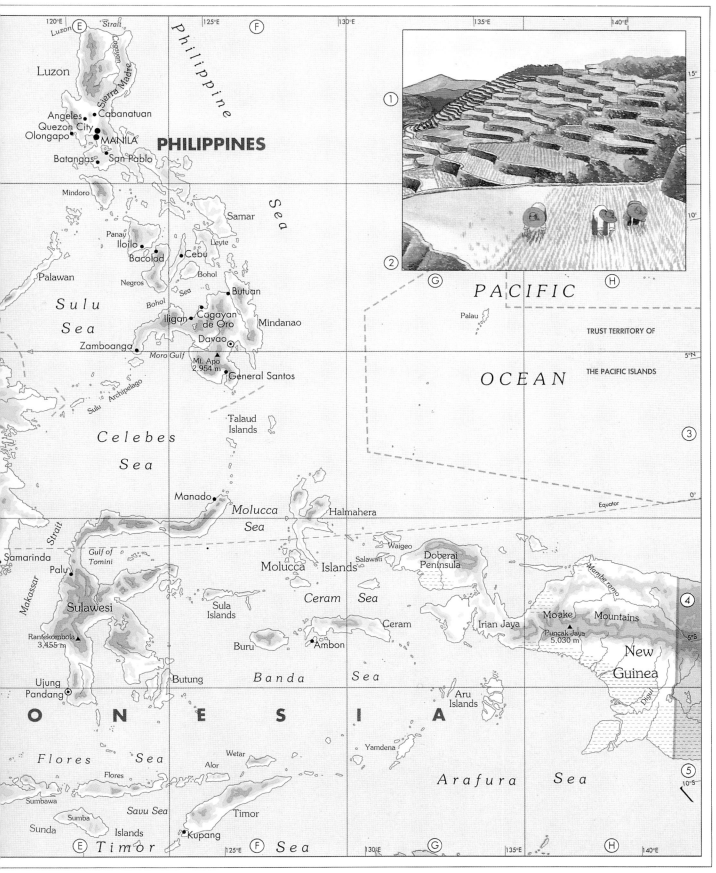

PHILIPPINES

Luzon

Angeles • Cabanatuan
Quezon City •
Olongapo • • MANILA
Batangas • • San Pablo

Mindoro

Samar

Panay
Iloilo •
Bacolod • Cebu

Leyte

Palawan

Negros

Bohol

Bohol
Sea • Butuan

Sulu Sea

Iligan • Cagayan de Oro
Zamboanga • Davao ⊙   Mindanao
Moro Gulf   Mt. Apo 2,954 m ▲
Sulu Archipelago   • General Santos

Celebes Sea

Talaud Islands

Manado •
Molucca Sea   Halmahera

Samarinda
Palu •   Gulf of Tomini
Molucca Islands
Sula Islands   *Ceram Sea*
Sulawesi   Ceram   Irian Jaya   Moake Mountains
Rantekombola 3,455 m ▲   Buru   Ambon   Puncak Jaya 5,030 m ▲   New Guinea

Ujung Pandang ⊙   Butung   *Banda Sea*   Aru Islands

O N E S I A

Flores Sea   Wetar   Yamdena
Flores   Alor
Sumbawa   Timor
Sumba   Savu Sea   *Arafura Sea*
Sunda   Islands   Kupang
E   *T i m o r*   *Sea*

Philippine Sea

PACIFIC   Palau

OCEAN   TRUST TERRITORY OF   THE PACIFIC ISLANDS

Equator

EAST ASIA

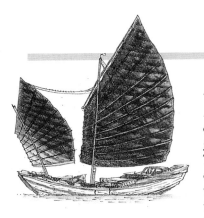

Traditional Boats
Traditional Chinese junks are still used for fishing in the coastal waters, though today most of them have motors as well as sails.

Buddhism
Buddhism reached China and Japan from India. About one in five of all the people in the world follow the teachings of Buddha.

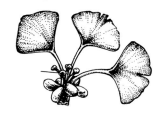

Ancient Trees
Wild ginkgo, or maidenhair, trees grow in one tiny area of China. They are grown for their fruits, timber, and oil.

The Great Wall of China
The Great Wall of China is about 1,500 miles long. Built to keep out warring Tatar tribes, it was completed in 214 BC.

East Asia is dominated by China, the third largest country in the world. There are great variations in its landscape. The Tibetan highlands are a cold plateau bordered by towering mountains, whereas the fertile Southern Uplands have a tropical climate.

Mongolia is a high plateau rising to mountains in the west with the "singing sands" of the Gobi Desert in the south.

To the east lie Korea and the volcanic islands of Japan and Taiwan. These are some of the most industrialized nations in the world.

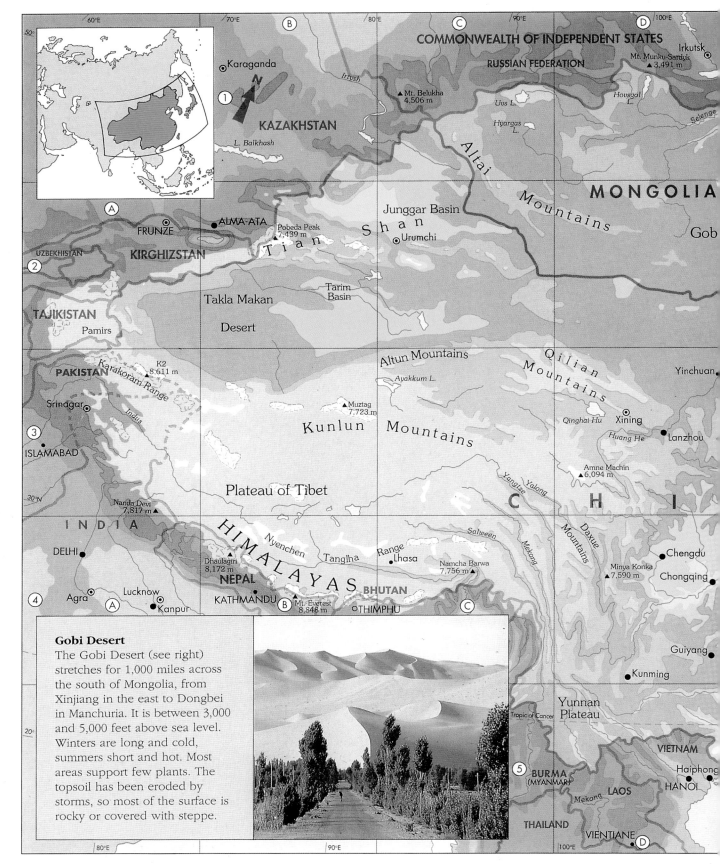

Gobi Desert
The Gobi Desert (see right) stretches for 1,000 miles across the south of Mongolia, from Xinjiang in the east to Dongbei in Manchuria. It is between 3,000 and 5,000 feet above sea level. Winters are long and cold, summers short and hot. Most areas support few plants. The topsoil has been eroded by storms, so most of the surface is rocky or covered with steppe.

Potala Palace

Potala Palace at Lhasa was built for the Dalai Lama. He was the Supreme Ruler of Tibet until China invaded in 1950.

Panda

The giant panda lives high in the mountains of southwestern China and eastern Tibet. It is now endangered and 12 panda reserves have been set up to protect these delightful creatures.

The World's Largest City

Tokyo, the capital of Japan, is the world's largest city. It has a population of over 25 million (see left).

Seoul

Seoul, the capital of South Korea, has spread far outside the ancient walls with their eight gateways (see below).

FACT CHART

● The Yangtze, China's longest river and the third longest in the world, flows 3,400 miles from Tibet to the East China Sea.

● The Huang He flows for 2,900 miles from the Kunlun Mountains to the Yellow Sea.

● Fujiyama, at 12,388 feet, is the highest peak in Japan. The last eruption of this volcano was in 1707.

● China's population is about 1,115,883,000 – over 20 percent of the world's total.

● Japan's islands average 1,500 earthquakes a year, but most are only slight tremors. There are also 150 volcanoes, of which 60 are active.

● Japan has the world's longest railway tunnel under the mountains – the Oshimuzu tunnel (nearly 14 miles long).

● China's Grand Canal is about 1,118 miles long and can carry ships of up to 2,200 tons.

● The highest peak in North Korea is Mount Paektu-san (9,003 feet). Mount Halla-san (6,398 feet), an extinct volcano, is the highest in South Korea.

Scale approximately 1:16,667,000
At the scale of this map the straight line distance from Hong Kong (E5) to Tokyo (H3) is approximately 1,797 miles (2,893 km).

OCEANIA

Oceania takes its name from the Pacific Ocean, the vast expanse of water that lies between Asia and the Americas. The continent is often called Australasia. Australia, a land of forests, deserts, and scrub, is the largest country in the region. It has a unique wildlife.

To the north, across the Torres Strait, lies Papua-New Guinea, a land of remote mountains and tropical forests. The twin islands of New Zealand lie to the southeast of Australia. Thousands of other tiny islands are scattered eastwards across the Pacific.

Gum Trees

The Sydney blue gum tree is one of the many eucalyptus trees of Australia. These tall, broadleaved evergreens provide timber and oil.

Coral Reefs

The northeastern coast of Australia is shielded by the world's largest expanse of coral. This Great Barrier Reef is 1,256 miles long.

FACT CHART

● Australasia is the smallest continent covering only 6 percent of the earth.

● The original inhabitants of Oceania include the Aborigines of Australia, and the Melanesians, Micronesians, and Polynesians of the Pacific islands. The Maoris of New Zealand are just one of the many Polynesian peoples.

● The highest point in the region is Mount Wilhelm (14,793 feet) in Papua-New Guinea.

● Lake Eyre in Australia is the largest lake in the region (3,436 sq. miles).

● The oldest known rocks (4,300 million years) come from near Perth.

● In ancient times the inhabitants of Oceania were the world's greatest seafarers. The Lapita people, ancestors of today's islanders, settled almost 8 million square miles of the Pacific between about 1500 BC and AD 1000. They used sailing canoes.

Honey Possums

The honey possum (see right) has a long, brush-tipped tongue which it uses to sip nectar from flowers, especially banksias. This tiny creature lives in trees and keeps its young in a pouch, like kangaroos.

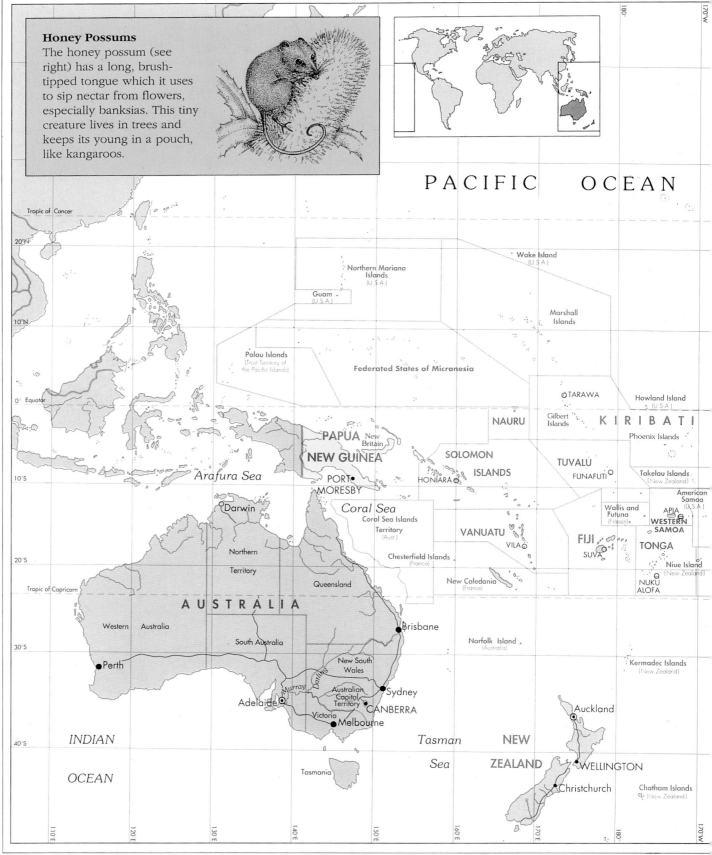

Strange Nature

The platypus (see left) is a strange-looking creature that lives in Australian rivers. It belongs to a small group of mammals, called monotremes, which lay eggs. Australia has many unique mammals. Some, such as kangaroos, koalas, and wombats, are marsupials. Their young are protected by a special pouch on the bodies of their mothers.

The Great Dividing Range

The main mountain range runs down eastern Australia from Queensland to Victoria. This range (see left) includes the beautiful Australian Alps and the Blue Mountains. There are smaller ranges in other regions, but none of them are over 5,000 feet.

New Zealand Southern Beech

New Zealand has almost 17 million acres of forest. The 90-feet-high southern beech grows in the wetter regions.

Pacific Islands

Most Pacific islands are formed from volcanic rock and coral. Many of the local people, like this woman at a cultural center in Fiji, practice traditional crafts.

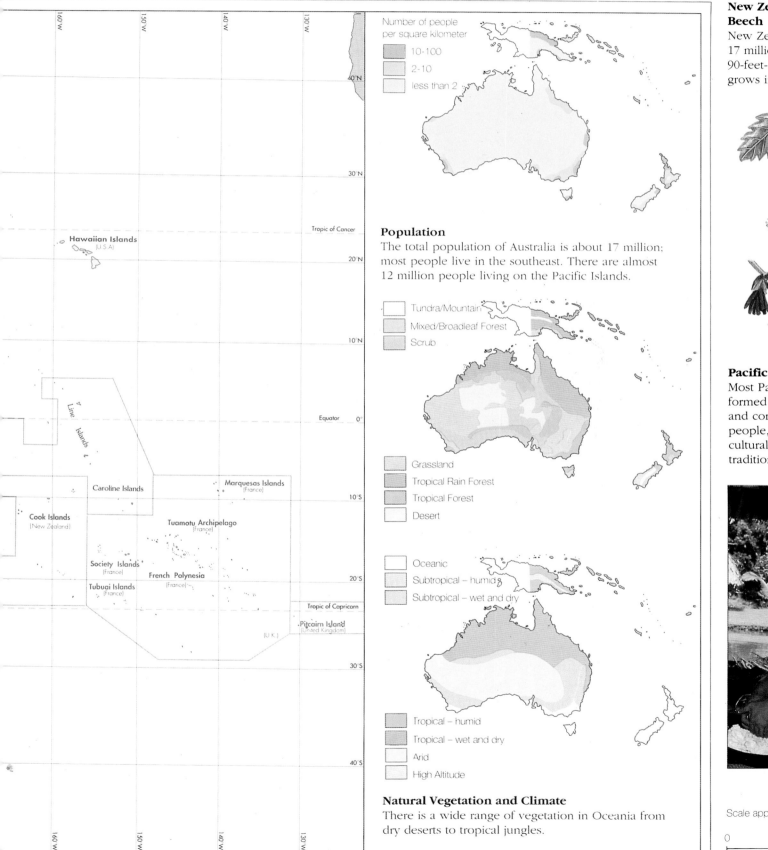

Number of people per square kilometer

- 10-100
- 2-10
- less than 2

Population

The total population of Australia is about 17 million; most people live in the southeast. There are almost 12 million people living on the Pacific Islands.

- Tundra/Mountain
- Mixed/Broadleaf Forest
- Scrub
- Grassland
- Tropical Rain Forest
- Tropical Forest
- Desert
- Oceanic
- Subtropical – humid
- Subtropical – wet and dry
- Tropical – humid
- Tropical – wet and dry
- Arid
- High Altitude

Natural Vegetation and Climate

There is a wide range of vegetation in Oceania from dry deserts to tropical jungles.

Hawaiian Islands (U.S.A.)

Line Islands

Caroline Islands

Marquesas Islands (France)

Cook Islands (New Zealand)

Tuamotu Archipelago (France)

Society Islands (France)

French Polynesia

Tubuai Islands (France)

Pitcairn Island (United Kingdom) (U.K.)

Tropic of Cancer

Equator

Tropic of Capricorn

Scale approximately 1:48,550,000

0   1,000   2,000 km

0   500   1,000 miles

AUSTRALIA

Australia is the sixth largest country in the world. It is mostly a land of burning deserts and dry scrub. In the far east there are more fertile regions, where crops are grown and cattle and sheep raised. It is in this area that the largest cities have grown up.

Australia is divided into six states and two territories. The national capital is at Canberra, but the largest city is Sydney, in New South Wales.

Australia's First Inhabitants
Many Aborigines, the first settlers in Australia, still try to follow the ancient traditions of their people.

Wildlife
Because of Australia's long isolation from other lands, it has many unique animals. Kangaroos (see above) and kookaburras (see below) are celebrated in Australian folk songs and tales.

City Skyline
Australia's finest modern building is the Sydney Opera House (see below), which has a beautiful harbor.

FACT CHART

● The Murray-Darling (2,330 miles) is the longest river.

● Cloncurry in Queensland holds Australia's temperature record – 127.6°F.

● Only 13 percent of Australia is above 1,640 feet high. The highest point is Mount Kosciusko at over 7,300 feet.

● Australia's Great Barrier Reef, the largest in the world, stretches 1,200 miles along the coast and is over 1,650 feet thick.

Scale approximately 1:23,530,000
At the scale of this map the straight line distance from Perth (A4) to Brisbane (D3) is approximately 2,237 miles (3,600 km).

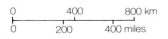

0   400   800 km
0   200   400 miles

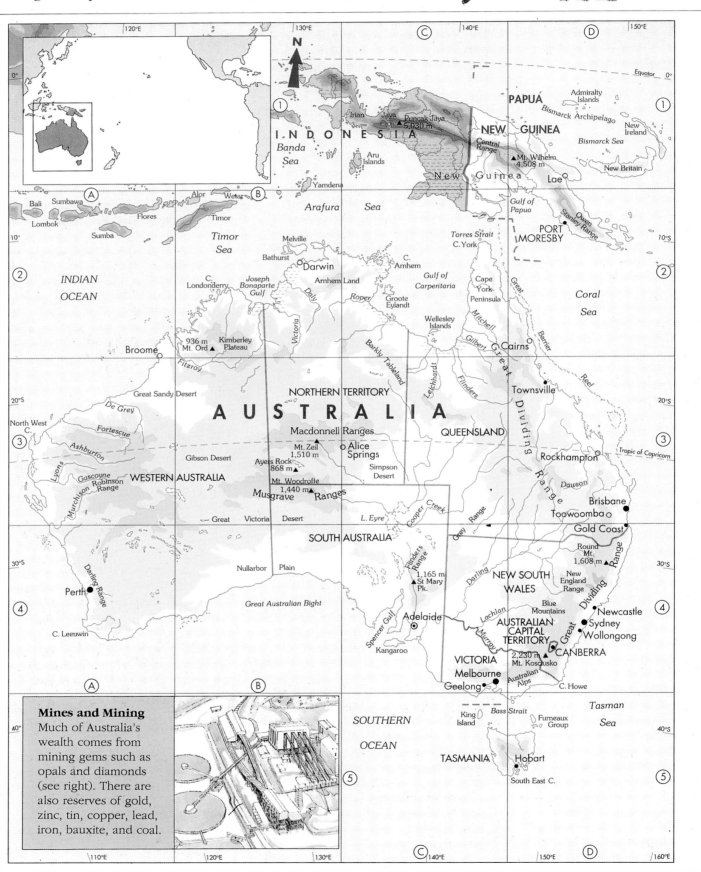

Mines and Mining
Much of Australia's wealth comes from mining gems such as opals and diamonds (see right). There are also reserves of gold, zinc, tin, copper, lead, iron, bauxite, and coal.

NEW ZEALAND

Sheep Farming
For each human being in New Zealand, there are 20 sheep! The countryside provides ideal pasture, and New Zealand is famous for its lamb.

New Zealand consists of two major islands – North Island and South Island – and several smaller ones. A mountain range, the Southern Alps, run the length of South Island with flat, fertile plains stretching to the east coast. North Island has fertile grazing land and a central plateau with active volcanoes. Sheep and dairy farming provide the main exports. Forestry and fishing are becoming increasingly important industries.

The Tuatara
The tuatara (see right) is the only reptile of its kind to survive into modern times. It lives only on offshore islands.

Kauri Forests
The lowlands of North Island support forests of kauri pines. These trees can grow to be 150 feet high with a diameter of up to 23 feet. Their gummy resin is used in varnishes. Some of these pines are 4,000 years old.

FACT CHART

● Twenty peaks of the Southern Alps exceed 10,000 feet – the highest is Mount Cook (12,352 feet).

● The kiwi – an unusual flightless bird – is the national symbol of New Zealand.

● Lake Taupo (234 sq. miles) is the largest lake.

● The Waikato River (264 miles) is the longest river.

● The Maoris, the first settlers, probably arrived in New Zealand about 1,000 years ago.

A Green Land
New Zealand's climate is ideal for growing a multitude of flowers (see left).

Scale approximately 1:6,666,000
At the scale of this map the straight line distance from Auckland (C2) to Dunedin (B5) is approximately 445 miles (717 km).

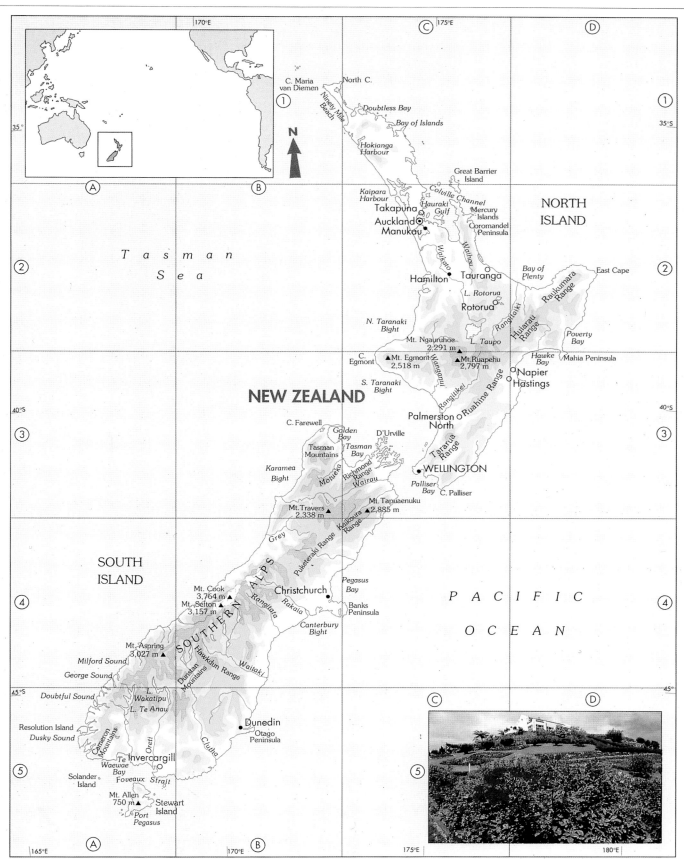

THE AMERICAS

Rain Forests in Danger
The extensive rain forests of Brazil are being threatened by loggers, farmers, and road builders.

San Francisco
The cosmopolitan city of San Francisco is the financial and cultural center of the western states (see below).

The landmass of the Americas stretches from the ice floes of the Arctic Ocean to the wild, windswept wilderness of Cape Horn. It forms two very different continents joined only by a narrow strip of land, the Isthmus of Panama.

The lands in between vary from rolling grasslands, great mountain ranges, and tropical forests to deserts. They include some of the richest and some of the poorest nations on Earth. The gleaming skyscrapers of Toronto or New York City in North America contrast with the flimsy shacks of shanty towns of Mexico City and Rio de Janeiro.

Native American peoples crossed into the continent from Siberia perhaps 15,000 or more years ago. They slowly settled throughout the continent. Great civilizations developed in Mexico and in the Andes, over thousands of years.

From the 1500s onwards, Europeans began to explore and colonize the land. Today, the Americas are home to a great mixture of cultures from all over the world.

The Canadian Rockies
The mighty range of the Rocky Mountains (see right) runs through British Columbia and Alberta before crossing the United States border.

Scale approximately 1:48,550,000

```
0        1,000        2,000 km
0      500      1,000 miles
```

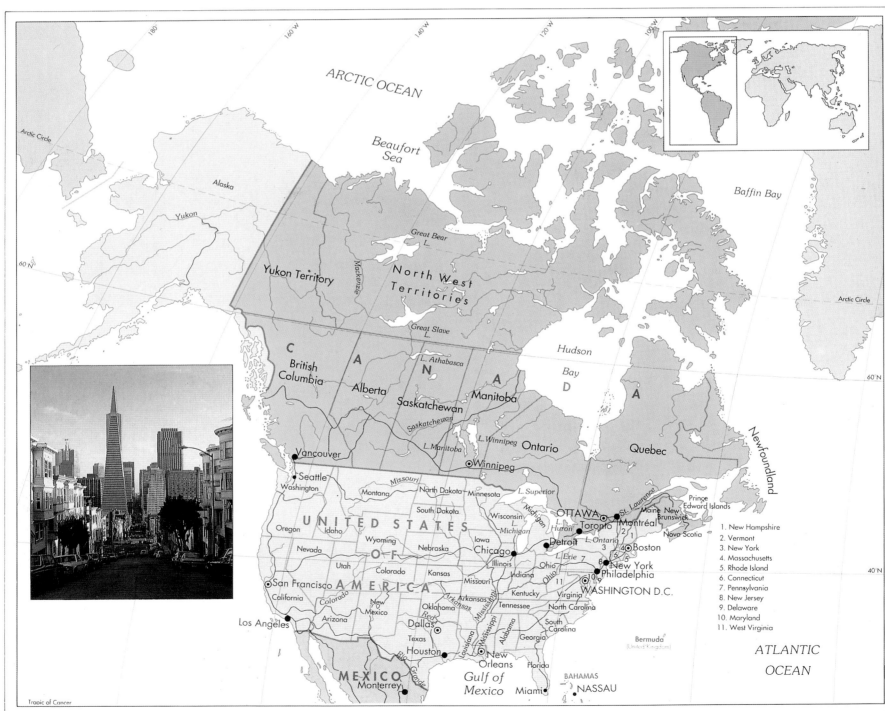

1. New Hampshire
2. Vermont
3. New York
4. Massachusetts
5. Rhode Island
6. Connecticut
7. Pennsylvania
8. New Jersey
9. Delaware
10. Maryland
11. West Virginia

F A C T   C H A R T

● North America includes the world's second largest country (Canada) and the fourth largest (the United States). The border between the two is the longest in the world (almost 3,990 miles).

● Only the Panama Canal, opened to shipping in 1914, divides North and South America.

● The San Andreas Fault, one of the world's most active earthquake zones, runs through California.

● The Gulf of Mexico is noted for its terrible hurricanes, whirling storms which often devastate the area.

● Chile's Atacama Desert is said to be the driest place on Earth. The wettest place is probably Tutunendo, in Colombia, with an average rainfall of 456 inches each year.

The Mexican Desert
In the deserts of Mexico, the saguaro cactus and prickly pear survive by storing water in their stems. Their sharp spines prevent them from being eaten.

The Caribbean
Blue seas, white sands, and palm trees attract tourists from all over the world to Caribbean islands such as St. Lucia (see above).

Spanish Influence
Córdoba in Argentina shares its name and its style of architecture with Córdoba in Spain. The influence of colonists can be seen in local architecture throughout the Americas (see above).

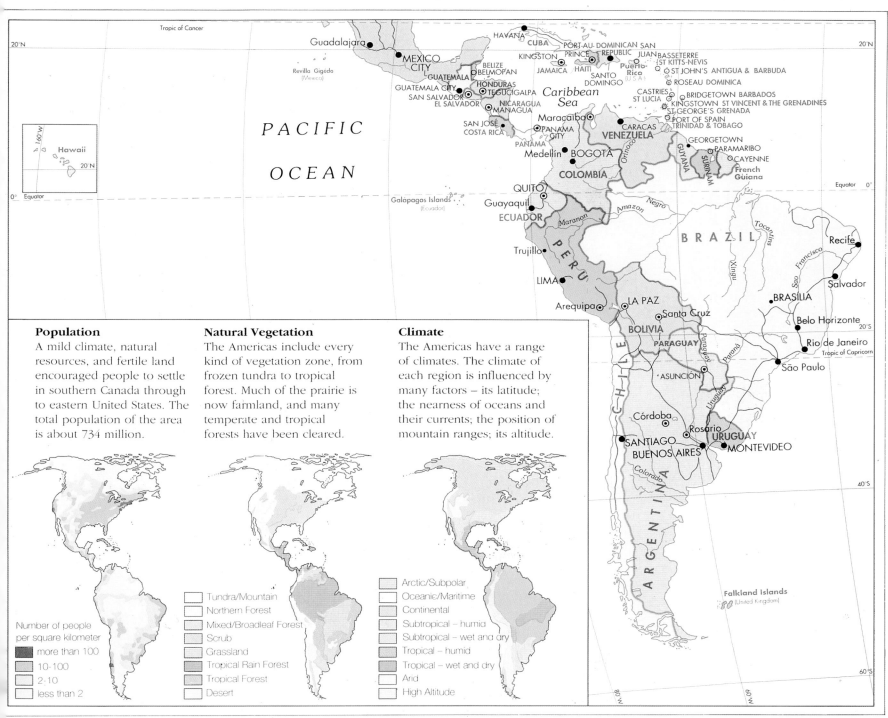

Population
A mild climate, natural resources, and fertile land encouraged people to settle in southern Canada through to eastern United States. The total population of the area is about 734 million.

Natural Vegetation
The Americas include every kind of vegetation zone, from frozen tundra to tropical forest. Much of the prairie is now farmland, and many temperate and tropical forests have been cleared.

Climate
The Americas have a range of climates. The climate of each region is influenced by many factors – its latitude; the nearness of oceans and their currents; the position of mountain ranges; its altitude.

Number of people per square kilometer
- more than 100
- 10-100
- 2-10
- less than 2

- Tundra/Mountain
- Northern Forest
- Mixed/Broadleaf Forest
- Scrub
- Grassland
- Tropical Rain Forest
- Tropical Forest
- Desert

- Arctic/Subpolar
- Oceanic/Maritime
- Continental
- Subtropical – humid
- Subtropical – wet and dry
- Tropical – humid
- Tropical – wet and dry
- Arid
- High Altitude

CANADA

anada's far north is an Arctic wilderness, with vast areas of frozen tundra and pine forests, icy mountains and lonely lakes. Most Canadians live in the south of the country, which has a milder climate. The large cities of the southeast include Toronto, Ottawa, Quebec, and Montréal.

The mid-western provinces of Canada are mainly vast prairies used to raise cattle and wheat. Sawmills and lumber camps provide work in the west. Most of the sawmills are sited on the large rivers in the area. Vancouver is Canada's chief port on the Pacific coast.

Lodgepole Pine
The lodgepole (see above) grows on the slopes of the Canadian Rockies. Its long trunk was used by North American Indians as a support pole for their lodges, or teepees.

French Canada
The imposing Château Frontenac (see above) is not in France but in Québec. It was built by the Canadian Pacific Railway. The French founded Québec in 1608 and it is still French-speaking.

Toronto
Although Ottawa is Canada's capital, Toronto (see above) is its largest city, with 3½ million inhabitants. A center of business and industry, it has many modern buildings.

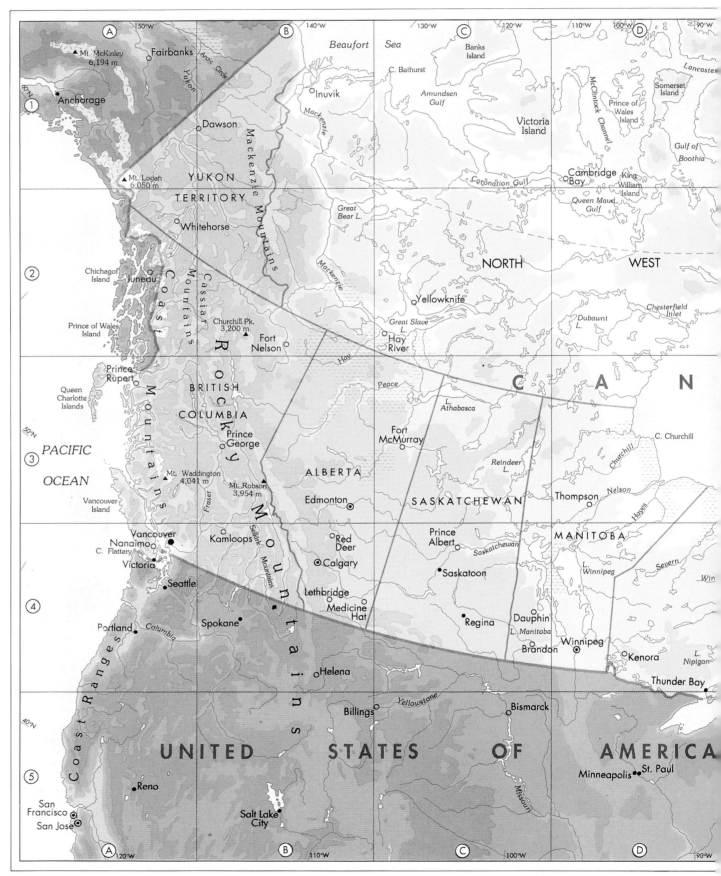

44

Native Americans

A traditional totem pole of carved wood (see left), painted and decorated with animals, watches over an Indian village on Canada's Pacific coast. The first people to live in Canada and the US were American Indians. Although Native Americans are now out numbered by 100 to one, many of them maintain their traditions with pride.

Animals of the Forest

Much of the coniferous forests of central Canada are still unspoilt. Animals such as moose, deer, bears, and wolves (see left) roam in them.

A Visitor's Paradise

Money from tourism is vital to Canada's economy. One of the top ten countries for holidays, people enjoy Canada's scenery (see below) and outdoor sports.

The Inuit

Inuits, meaning "the People", now live in modern cabins rather than their traditional tents of caribou skin (see above). However, some Inuit still build traditional igloos from snow blocks (see below) when on hunting expeditions.

F A C T   C H A R T

● Canada is made up of 10 provinces and two territories. The least populated regions are Yukon and Northwest Territories. The most crowded provinces are Ontario and Québec.

● The highest mountain in Canada is Mount Logan in Yukon (19,524 feet).

● The longest river in Canada is the Mackenzie (2,630 miles).

● Canada has over one million lakes – more than the rest of the world combined.

● The largest lake entirely in Canada is the Great Bear Lake (12,270 sq. miles).

● Canada is rich in oil and natural gas. The Trans-Canada gas pipeline is the world's longest (over 6,590 miles).

● Canada's national game is ice hockey, which was probably first played in 1855 at Kingston, Ontario.

● The Royal Canadian Mounted Police, founded in 1873, is one of the world's most famous forces. It was said that the daring "Mounties" always got their man.

● Canada has many mineral resources including copper, zinc, nickel, iron ore, gold, and lead.

Scale approximately 1:15,789,000
At the scale of this map the straight line distance from Vancouver (A4) to Quebec (F4) is approximately 2,361 miles (3,802 km).

The Bald Eagle
The national symbol of the United States, the bald eagle, is now an endangered species and protected in many areas.

The Island State
Hawaii, the last state to join the Union in 1959, is made up of 130 islands in the Pacific Ocean 2,083 miles west of California. The palm-fringed beaches and tropical climate makes Hawaii a favorite holiday resort.

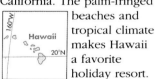

Scale approximately 1:48,550,000 (for Hawaii map only)

Scale approximately 1:12,000,000 At the scale of this map the straight line distance from Seattle (A1) to New York (H2) is approximately 2,407 miles (3,876 km).

```
0       200      400   500 km
0       100      200      300 miles
```

The United States of America, one of the richest countries in the world, is so vast from west to east that it spans four different time zones. It is rich in natural resources with huge deposits of raw materials including oil, coal, natural gas, iron, and copper.

The fertile Great Plains that lie between the Rockies in the west and the Appalachians in the east make American farmers world leaders in agricultural produce. They export huge quantities of maize, citrus fruits, meat, milk, and wheat – one-fifth the value of all exports.

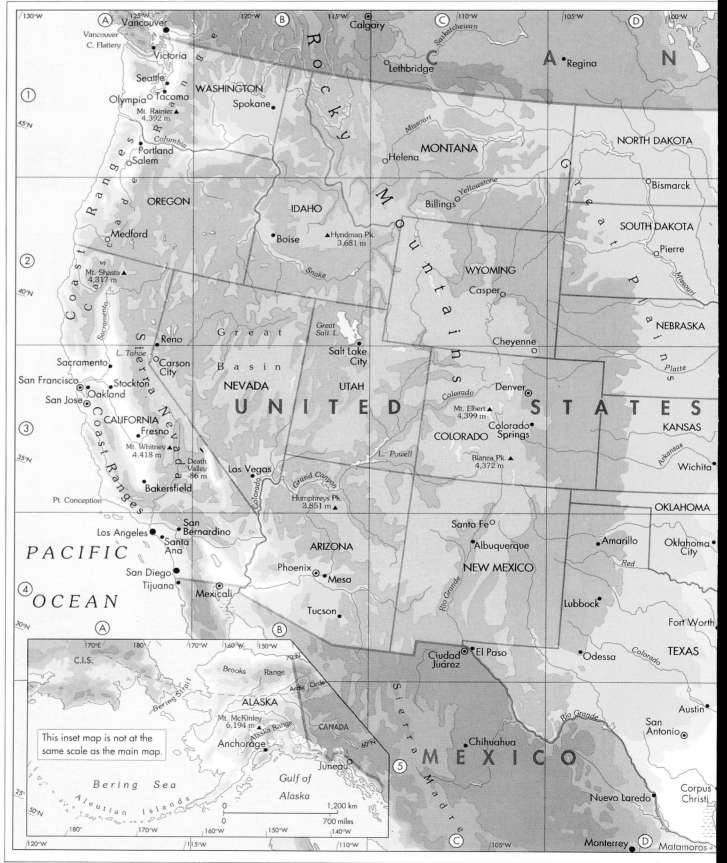

The Grand Canyon

Large rivers flowing across the Colorado Plateau in the southwest United States have carved huge canyons into the rock. These canyons are famous for their fantastic shapes and colors.

The Grand Canyon (see left) is over 250 miles long and between .12 and 18 miles wide; at points it towers 4,875 feet above the Colorado River.

The White House

The White House, a large mansion in Washington (see right), is the official home and office of the President of the United States.

New York City

The historic city of New York is world famous for its Manhattan skyline of towering skyscrapers (see below), especially the Empire State Building.

FACT CHART

● The fourth largest country in the world, the United States has almost 4.5 million miles of roads – nearly a third of a million miles are major highways and motorways.

● The Mississippi River, the longest river in North America, plus its main tributaries, the Missouri and the Ohio, drain all or part of 31 states and two Canadian provinces.

● There are 50 states, each with its own capital. The seven largest in population are California, New York, Texas, Florida, Pennsylvania, Illinois, and Ohio.

● The Stars and Stripes, the red stands for courage, the blue for justice and the white for liberty. The thirteen stripes represent the original colonies and the 50 stars the present day states.

● The national capital, Washington, lies in a specially created area – the District of Columbia – so that it is not allied to any one state.

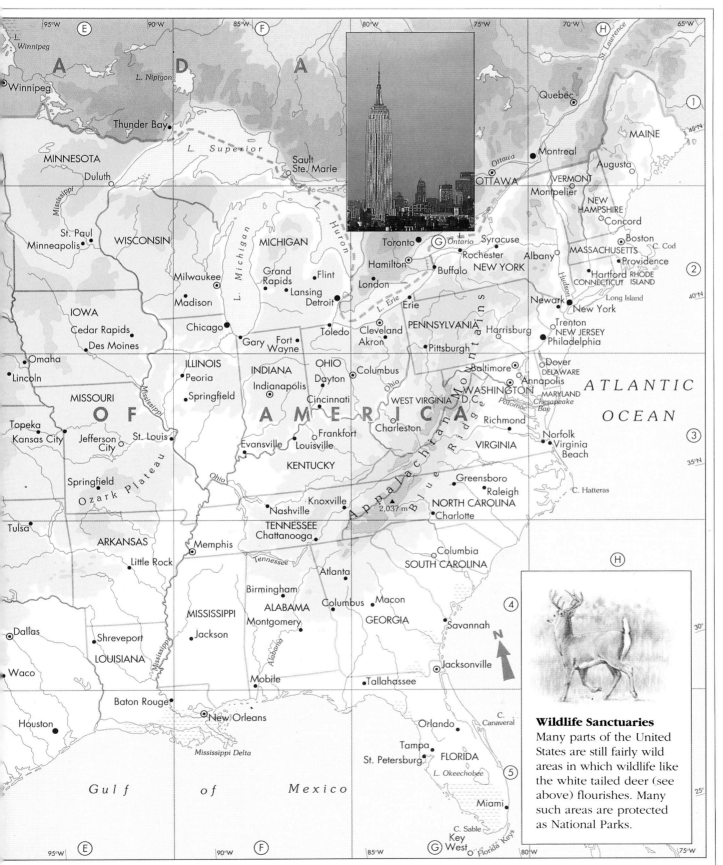

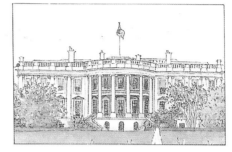

Wildlife Sanctuaries
Many parts of the United States are still fairly wild areas in which wildlife like the white tailed deer (see above) flourishes. Many such areas are protected as National Parks.

The World's Oldest Trees
Some giant sequoias (see above) are 3,000 to 4,000 years old – the world's largest and oldest living things.

47

Tropical Crops
Many Central American and Caribbean countries rely on crops such as bananas, sugar cane, and coffee.

Hurricane Damage
Tropical storms can gust at 186 miles an hour in the Caribbean, ripping up trees and houses in their path (see above).

Strange Homes
Nesting holes made by the galia woodpecker in a saguaro cactus of Mexican and Central American deserts are taken over by tiny elf owls (see above).

A Staple Food
Beans of many kinds are one of the main food crops of Mexico. Beans are served with chilis and *tortillas* (cornmeal pancakes).

The North American continent curves and narrows to the south. Mexico is the largest country in the region. North Mexico has deserts and a high plateau between two mountain ranges. To the south lie the small countries of Central America – Guatemala, Belize, El Salvador, Honduras, Nicaragua, Costa Rica, and Panama.

To the east are the long island chains of the Caribbean Sea – the Bahamas, and the Greater and Lesser Antilles.

Cuban Fishermen
Cuba is the largest Caribbean island. Fishing provides an important export.

World of the Maya
The ancient Maya lived in Yucatán and Guatemala. They built marvelous temples, the ruins of which can be seen throughout the region (see above). The Mayan civilization lasted from about 300 BC until 1519.

Caribbean Homes
Many Caribbean nations are poor, and their homes in the villages (see left) are often simple wooden shacks with tin roofs.

Capital of Belize
In 1961 a hurricane devastated the coast of Belize. It was decided to rebuild a modern capital, Belmopan (see right), 50 miles inland.

Endangered Turtles
Rare marine turtles such as the leatherback, the green (see above), and the hawksbill breed on the beaches of Costa Rica.

The Bahamas
The beautiful islands of the Bahamas with their waterfront markets (see left), are popular with tourists.

FACT CHART

● Citlaltepetl (18,697 feet), the highest peak in Mexico, is always covered in snow.

● Mexico City, one of the most crowded cities in the world, will probably have a population of over 24 million by the year 2000.

● Guatemala is the most populated Central American country with 9 million people. Belize is the least populated with 193,000.

● The Bahamas consist of 3,000 coral islands of which only 20 are inhabited.

● Tajumulco, a volcano in Guatemala, is the highest point in Central America (13,810 feet).

● The Panama Canal was completed in 1914. It is used as a short cut between the Pacific and Atlantic Oceans.

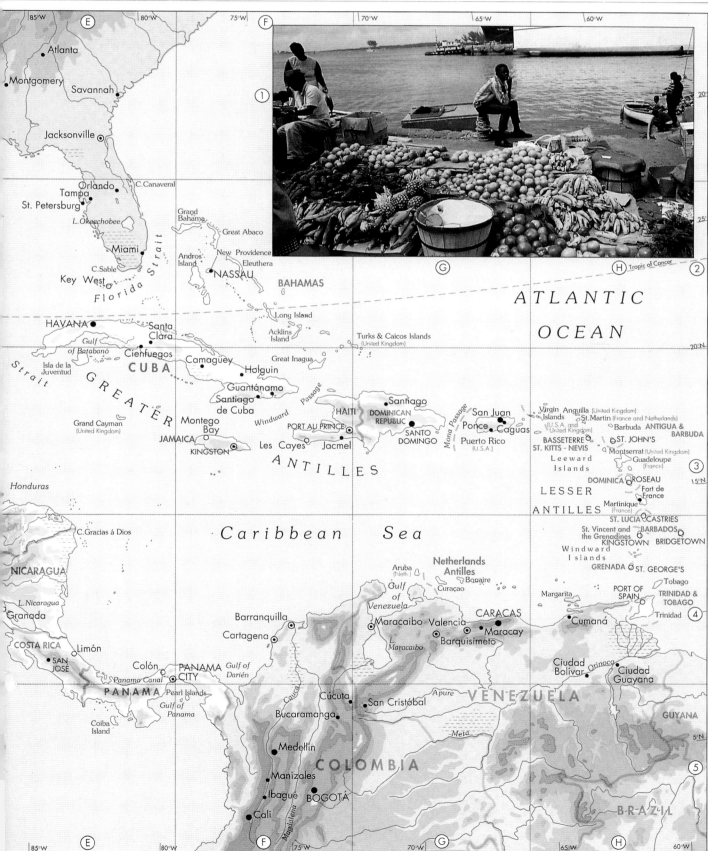

Antigua
Antigua, in the Lesser Antilles, with its sandy beaches and blue sea is a haven for holidaymakers.

Scale approximately 1:15,000,000
At the scale of this map the straight line distance from Guatemala City (D4) to Bridgetown (H4) is approximately 2,075 miles (3,342 km).

The Andes mountain range, which dominates Ecuador in northwest South America, continues into Colombia and Venezuela. To the east and west of the Andes lie dense rain forests which extend northwards from the Amazon basin. The flat coastal regions of Venezuela take in the vast, swampy delta of the Orinoco.

The landscape varies from the coastal strip of Guyana, where sea walls, dykes, and canals help to keep the water out, to the forested mountains of Surinam. Much of the interior of French Guiana is a wilderness.

Sugar Cane
The tropical climate of Guyana makes it ideal for growing sugar cane and there are large plantations. One region, Demerara, has given its name to a kind of brown sugar.

FACT CHART

● The light wood from balsa trees of the jungles of Ecuador was once used to make ocean-going rafts.

● Colombia's longest river is the Magdalena (965 miles).

● Over 80 percent of Surinam is covered by mountainous rain forest.

● The world's highest waterfall lies on a branch of the River Carrao in Venezuela. The Cherun-Meru, known in English as the Angel Falls, has a total height of 3,212 feet.

● Cotopaxi (19,344 feet) in Ecuador is the world's highest active volcano.

● Lake Maracaibo in Venezuela, one of the first areas to be developed for offshore oil production, is the largest in the region (5,150 sq. miles).

● The Andes are the longest mountain chain in the world – 4,500 miles.

● Devil's Island in French Guiana housed the world's most notorious prison until it was closed in 1945.

Scale approximately 1:10,127,000
At the scale of this map the straight line distance from Quito (B4) to Paramaribo (G2) is approximately 1,663 miles (2,678 km).

```
0        200      400 km
0    100      200 miles
```

Ecuador

Ecuador takes its name from the Equator, on which it lies. Most of the people live in the valleys. Cattle and sheep are raised and sold at market. This is often the women's job (see left).

Mining in French Guiana

Bauxite, the ore used to make aluminum, is mined in French Guiana, which has many mineral deposits.

Wildlife in Danger

Rain forest covers the interior of the region. It is a treasure house of animal species, including parrots and monkeys (see right and below). Many species are threatened by forest clearance for roads, farmland, and mining. River creatures, too, are in danger, including the boto, a river dolphin, and the black caiman.

Wealth from Oil

Venezuela has rich reserves of oil. Production is centered on the Maracaibo region. Further oil fields lie beneath the Orinoco basin and offshore below the Caribbean Sea. Large oil refineries (see below) attract many workers.

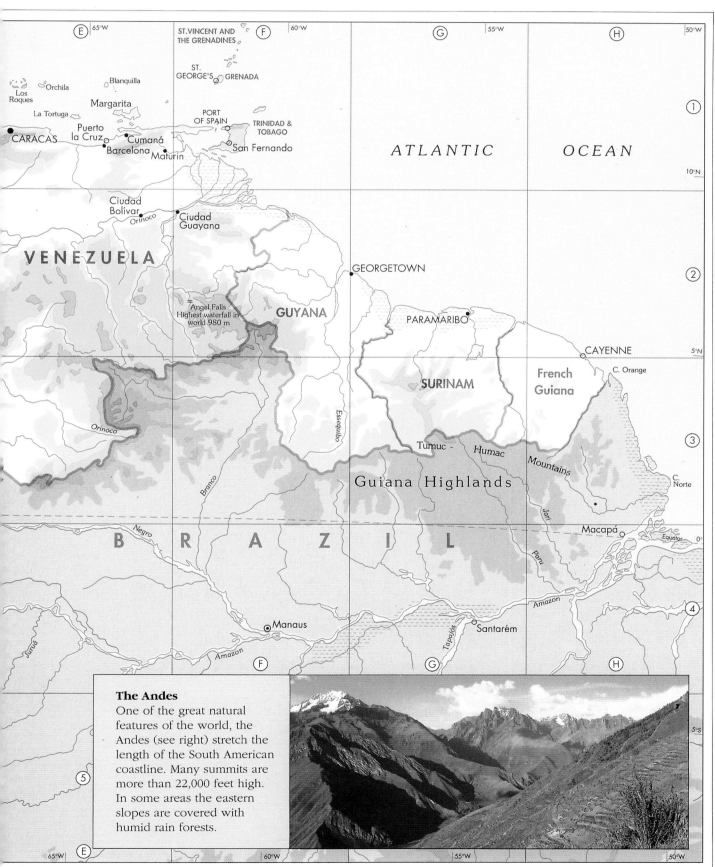

ST. VINCENT AND THE GRENADINES

Los Roques
Orchila
Blanquilla
Margarita
La Tortuga
ST. GEORGE'S — GRENADA
PORT OF SPAIN
TRINIDAD & TOBAGO
Puerto la Cruz
CARACAS
Cumaná
Barcelona
Maturín
San Fernando

ATLANTIC OCEAN

Ciudad Bolívar
Orinoco
Ciudad Guayana

VENEZUELA

GEORGETOWN

Angel Falls Highest waterfall in world 980 m

GUYANA

PARAMARIBO

CAYENNE
C. Orange

SURINAM

French Guiana

Orinoco
Essequibo

Tumuc - Humac Mountains
C. Norte

Guiana Highlands
Jari

Branco

Macapá
Equator

Negro

B R A Z I L

Amazon

Panu

Junua
Manaus
Santarém
Amazon
Tapajós

The Andes

One of the great natural features of the world, the Andes (see right) stretch the length of the South American coastline. Many summits are more than 22,000 feet high. In some areas the eastern slopes are covered with humid rain forests.

The high mountain chain of the Andes runs southwards through Peru, Bolivia, and Chile. Chile is 2,666 miles long but only 93–124 miles wide. The continent's largest country is Brazil, which takes in the vast Amazon basin, the highlands of the southeast, and the coastal cities. Paraguay and Uruguay are lands of fertile hills and plains, given over to farming. Argentina's grasslands, the *pampas*, are grazed by large herds of cattle. Further south lie the remote plateaus of the Patagonia region and the bleak wilderness of Tierra del Fuego.

Antarctic Beech

This tree braves the cold winds of the southern Andes and the remote islands of southern Chile. It can reach a height of 90 feet in more sheltered areas. It often grows alongside lenga and monkey-puzzle trees.

FACT CHART

● The Amazon is the second longest river in the world – 4,000 miles from the Peruvian Andes to the South Atlantic. The forests are home to many Amazon Indian Tribes.

● The Andes were home to many great civilizations, such as that of the Incas. Their empire, based around Cuzco, in Peru, flourished from 1300 until the Spanish invasion of 1532.

● Lake Titicaca in Bolivia and Peru is the largest lake in the region (3,220 sq. miles) and the highest navigable lake in the world.

● Mount Aconcagua in Argentina and Chile is the highest peak in the region (22,830 feet).

● Parts of the Atacama Desert in Chile have not had rain for over 400 years – it is the driest place on Earth.

Scale approximately 1:20,000,000
At the scale of this map the straight line distance from Belém (E1) to Montevideo (D5) is approximately 2,352 miles (3,787 km).

0	250	500	750 km
0		200	400 miles

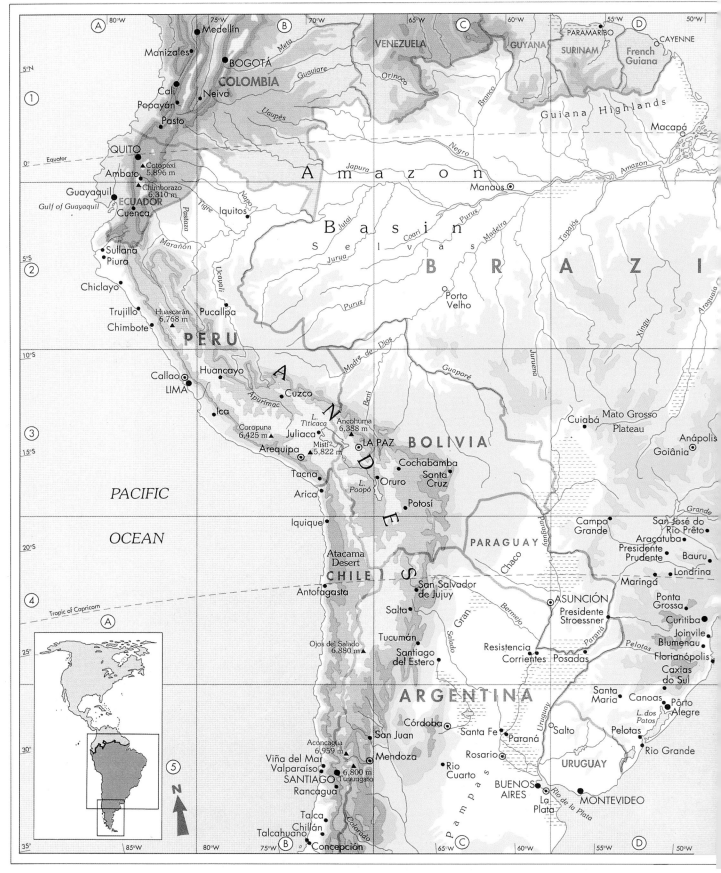

Brazilian Cowboys

Brazil, like Argentina, has large herds of beef and dairy cattle. These herds are tended by teams of cowboys on horses.

Buenos Aires

The capital of Argentina (see right), Buenos Aires lies on the banks of the Rio de la Plata. It was once the main port of Argentina.

Palm Huts

Throughout South America, shacks of palm leaves (see above) and wood or tin exist alongside modern skyscrapers of concrete and steel.

The Brazilian Forest

The Amazon rain forest is the largest in the world. Its clearance threatens wildlife (see above), plants, and the Indian tribes who live there.

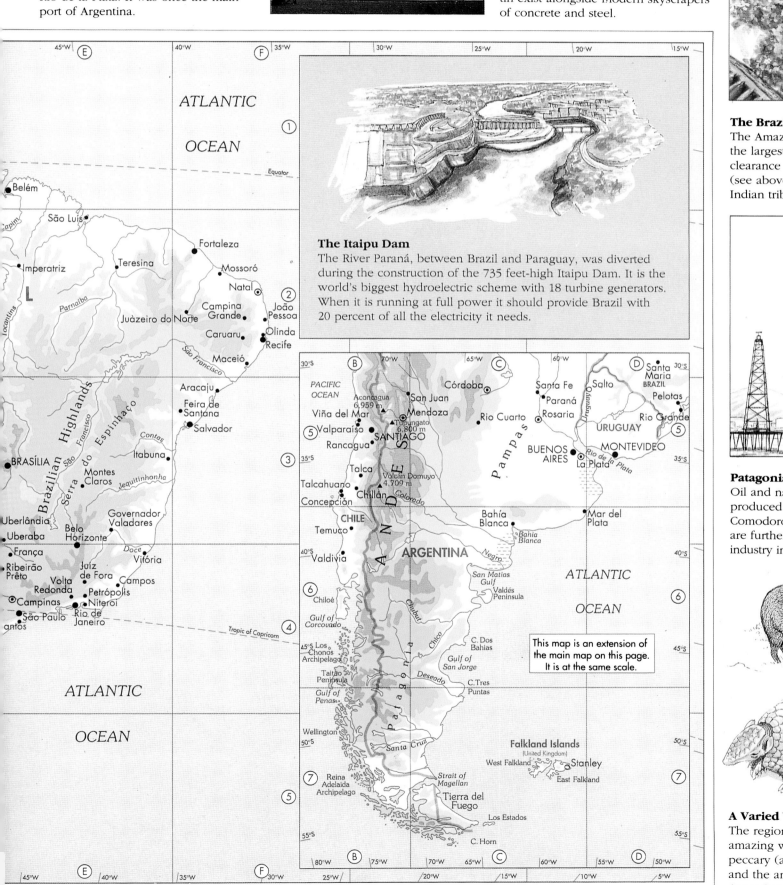

The Itaipu Dam

The River Paraná, between Brazil and Paraguay, was diverted during the construction of the 735 feet-high Itaipu Dam. It is the world's biggest hydroelectric scheme with 18 turbine generators. When it is running at full power it should provide Brazil with 20 percent of all the electricity it needs.

This map is an extension of the main map on this page. It is at the same scale.

Patagonian Oil

Oil and natural gas are produced at the port of Comodoro Rivadavia. There are further plans to develop industry in this remote region.

A Varied Wildlife

The region is famous for its amazing wildlife such as the peccary (a piglike animal) and the armadillo from Argentina (see above).

ARCTIC OCEAN

Animal Life

Polar bears (see below), which live on the Arctic tundra and ice floes are expert hunters. Their main food, seals (see above), live in the water and crawl out onto the ice to sunbathe.

FACT CHART

● At the North Pole, the sun does not rise above the horizon for six months of the year and it is dark all the time. For the other half of the year the sun never sets.

● The Arctic contains valuable minerals, including coal, oil, copper, nickel, iron, and gold.

● Sea temperatures average 32°F in July and −40°F in January.

● The first man to reach the North Pole was an American, Robert Peary. He traveled over the ice with teams of dogs in 1909.

● In 1958 the US nuclear-powered submarine *Nautilus* crossed the Arctic Ocean under the ice, passing the North Pole on the way.

Baffin Island

Baffin Island (see right) is a high plateau with mountains, glaciers, and snowfields rising to 8,000 feet. Part of it is protected as the Anyuittuq National Park.

Scale approximately 1:26,650,000
At the scale of this map the straight line distance from the North Pole (C2) to Jan Mayen (D4) is approximately 2,365 miles (3,806 km).

0	250	500	750 km
0	200		400 miles

The Arctic, the smallest of the world's major oceans, is 3,300 miles across, with the North Pole at the center. Most of the ocean is covered in ice. In some parts there are patchy ice floes 5 feet thick, with clear water between them. In other parts, the solid masses of ice are over 50 feet thick.

The Arctic is only about 17,850 feet at its deepest part. Areas of continental shelf project out from the surrounding landmasses. These are thought to contain large deposits of oil and minerals.

Right Whale

Whales have been hunted so much that their numbers have severely diminished. The Greenland and black right whale (see above) are slow-moving and easily captured. They are now protected species.

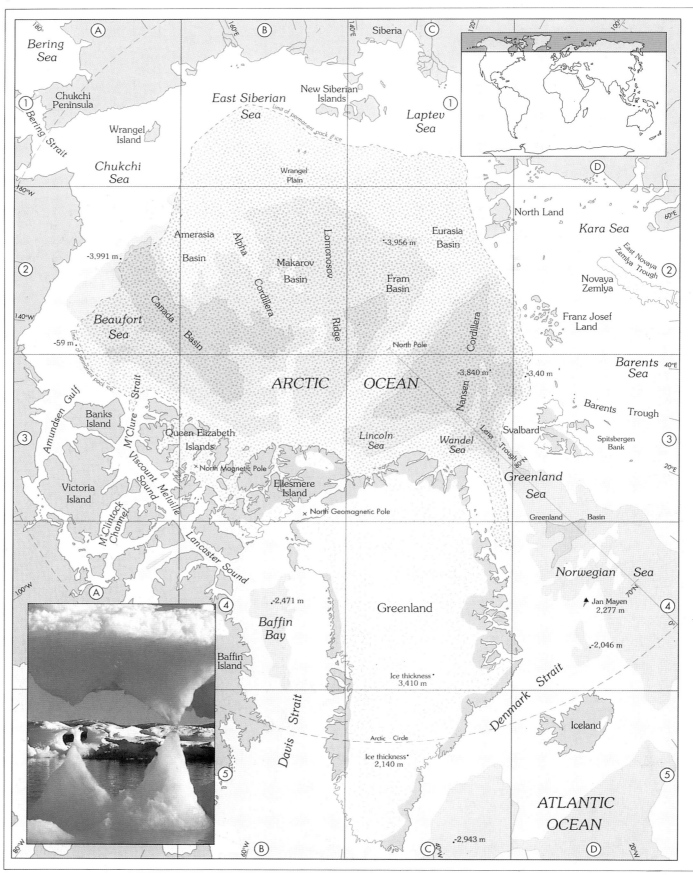

Blue Whale
The blue whale (see above), the largest animal in the world, can grow to 100 feet long and weigh up to 120 tons.

A Land of Ice
A very thick ice-cap covers Antarctica (see below), forming a vast plateau that rises to 9,000 feet.

Whereas the Arctic is an ocean surrounded by land, Antarctica is a continent ringed by water. The Southern Ocean is the world's stormiest ocean. Blizzards blow north at great speeds and can last for days.

Antarctica is much colder than the Arctic. For most of the year pack-ice covers the ocean's two main arms, the Weddell and Ross Seas. In summer many icebergs are released and float north to latitude 55°S and even further. The only humans in Antarctica are visiting scientists and explorers.

Cold Water Fish
There are few plants and no land animals in the Antarctic, but the ocean teems with life, including the antifreeze fish (see above) which can survive freezing temperatures.

Penguins
The emperor penguin (see above) is native to Antarctica. At 3 feet tall, it is the largest of the penguin species.

FACT CHART

● One of the biggest icebergs ever recorded in the Southern Ocean was the size of Belgium. Large bergs may drift in the ocean currents for many years, gradually being eroded into fantastic shapes.

● A record low temperature of −126°F was recorded at a research base on Antarctica.

● At the South Pole in central Antarctica the ice-cap is about 8,930 feet thick.

● The first person to reach the South Pole in 1911 was Roald Amundsen, a Norwegian. He was followed 35 days later by Captain Robert Scott leading a British expedition. Scott and his party died on the return journey.

● The Greenland glacier is the largest glacier in the Northern Hemisphere (700,000 sq. miles).

Scale approximately 1:22,700,000
At the scale of this map the straight line distance from the South Pole (B3) to the South Shetland Islands (B1) is approximately 2,352 miles (3,787 km)

| 0 | 500 | 1,000 km |
| 0 | 300 | 600 miles |

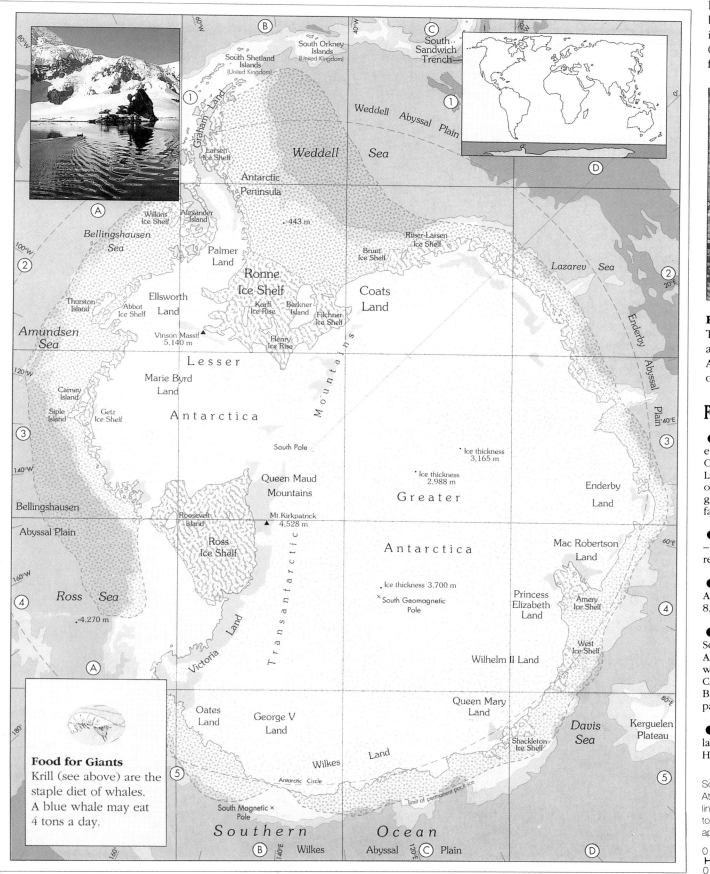

Food for Giants
Krill (see above) are the staple diet of whales. A blue whale may eat 4 tons a day.